Idea Bags for the Kitchen

Activities to Promote the School-to-Home Connection

by Sharon MacDonald
illustrated by Marilee Harrald-Pilz

Published by Fearon Teacher Aids
an imprint of

 **McGraw-Hill Children's Publishing**

Credits

Editorial Director: Hanna Otero

Editor: Lisa Trumbauer

Cover and Interior Design: Good Neighbor Press, Inc.

McGraw-Hill
Children's Publishing

A Division of The McGraw-Hill Companies

Published by Fearon Teacher Aids

An imprint of McGraw-Hill Children's Publishing

Copyright © 2002 McGraw-Hill Children's Publishing

Send all inquiries to:

McGraw-Hill Children's Publishing

3195 Wilson Drive NW

Grand Rapids, Michigan 49544

FE11036 Idea Bags for the Kitchen

ISBN: 0-7682-0733-9

1 2 3 4 5 6 7 8 9 07 06 05 04 03 02

Table of Contents

What's an Idea Bag?

An Idea Bag is a brown paper lunch bag filled with ideas parents can use at home to help further their child's learning. Idea Bags invite parents to do activities with their children to reinforce and expand concepts taught at school. The suggestions aim to capture parents' interest and involve them in a non-threatening way. Idea Bags allow parents to learn first, then teach their children.

Essential skills are sharpened through the activities. Children practice math when they measure ingredients and time cooking. They explore science when they observe how foods change while cooking. They expand language by learning cooking words, such as stir, pour, whip, and so on. They also learn sequencing and process skills as they follow directions.

The recipe on each bag cover lists the ingredients and necessary cooking needed. Parents will also find fun facts and questions to share with children. The sheet inside the bag gives step-by-step illustrated directions on one side, and suggested activities on the other. It also includes skills and new vocabulary.

Idea Bags can be sent home every other week during the school year; and seasonal recipes can be sent home at the appropriate time of year. For example, the "Roasted Corn" Idea Bag can be sent home in the fall.

Bon appétit!

 Idea Bags for the Kitchen FE11036

How to Make an Idea Bag

To make an Idea Bag, photocopy the recipe, and trim it to fit a brown paper lunchbag. Attach it to the outside of the bag using tape, glue, or a stapler. Then photocopy the step-by-step-directions page and activities page. Fold the sheets in the middle and slide them into the bag. If possible, make two-sided copies to save paper. You might ask parent volunteers or students from an upper grade to make photocopies and assemble the Idea Bags in advance. If parents offer to donate supplies, suggest a package of 50 or 100 lunch bags.

While Idea Bags are excellent tools for involving parents, they also fit easily into classroom study. During the fall season, for example, you can cook up several apple recipes in class. The ideas on the activity sheet can be incorporated into classroom study and discussion. If you decide not to send the Idea Bags home, you might consider adding the activities to your themed lessons.

When Idea Bags are sent home for the first time, include an introductory letter to the parents. This provides a brief explanation of the Idea Bags and defines expectations. Feel free to copy the parent letter on the next page, and change or rewrite it to suit your individual needs.

Idea Bags are not homework. Nothing needs to be returned to school. The kitchen activities in this book revolve around food preparation. They give parents the opportunity to facilitate learning in a pleasurable, familiar setting. The activities need not be completed precisely. Rather, the activities should be viewed as a chance for parents and children to bond and learn together.

Idea Bags offer a way for teachers to send home projects that are different from what parents are used to receiving from school. Many parents will find the Idea Bags interesting, helpful, and fun to use with their children.

Idea Bags are not a cure-all for getting parents involved. Some parents will use them, while others will not for a variety of reasons. Parents' time, priorities, energy, and attention are limited. As teachers, we can provide resources and encourage parents to use them. Do your best to reach as many as you can. That is what Idea Bags are all about.

Dear Parent(s):

Many of you have asked for ideas to do at home to help with your child's education. Today your child has brought home an Idea Bag. It contains a simple recipe, along with an activity sheet. Feel free to select one or all of the activities to enjoy with your child.

An Idea Bag gives you a chance to spend time with your child. The kitchen is a wonderful place to learn and explore, and an excellent place for you and your child to work and learn together. You might let your child do most of the cooking as you ask questions to guide and encourage your child's efforts. Invite your child to "read" the picture-directions and work at his or her own speed. As you and your child follow the recipe, share the fun facts and thought-provoking questions on the outside of the bag. Then engage your child in any of the activities on the sheet inside that sound interesting to you. The sheet also summarizes the skills and vocabulary your child will be practicing as you enjoy the cooking and the activities together.

This is NOT homework. Idea Bags are a resource of fun activities to do with your child. If your schedule is too busy this week, save the recipe activities for the weekend or next week. Involve others, like your child's baby-sitter, grandparents, or other friends or relatives who would enjoy completing some of the activities with your child. Many of the activities can also be done with children of different ages, so include other family members whenever possible. Invite your child's friends or relatives to join in the fun.

Most of the materials needed in the recipes are items that should be available in your kitchen. Some may need to be purchased. If you have trouble finding materials for a particular recipe, please let me know. We can help track down the items you need.

Idea Bags will be sent home about every two weeks. Enjoy cooking with your child and completing the activities. Your comments, ideas, and suggestions about the Idea Bags are welcome. Let me know how it's going.

Yours truly,

Apple Slices and Peanut Butter

Ingredients:

1 apple

peanut butter

Utensils:

an apple corer

a sharp knife (for adult use only)

a dull knife

a cutting board

The apple is the most widely grown of all fruits. It was among the first fruits eaten by early humans. The United States ranks second in the world in apple growing. Only China grows more. Different varieties of apples are ready to be picked every month of the year, although fall is traditionally apple-picking time.

Tip:

If your apple is brown or mealy, it is either too old or it has been stored incorrectly. Apples should be stored in a cool, dark place.

Did You Know:

You can fry apples! Fried apples will candy nicely if you put a bit of salt in the pan as you fry them.

Questions to ask while cooking:

1. Why do you think we remove the center, or core, of the apple?

2. How did the shape of the apple change when we sliced it?

3. Why do you think the peanut butter slides around when you try to spread it on the apple slice?

Cut along dashed line and glue to a brown paper lunch bag.

Idea Bags for the Kitchen FE11036

While preparing this recipe, your child is learning:

1. Fine-motor skills. These are the foundation for writing. Your child develops them when he or she holds and uses the knife for slicing and spreading. The same pincher control is necessary for holding a pencil. Slicing and spreading also requires good hand-eye coordination.

2. Science skills. Your child learns about cause and effect when trying to spread peanut butter on the slippery apple slice. What has caused the peanut butter to slip so easily?

3. Math skills. Slicing the apple provides an excellent opportunity to visit whole-part relationships, which are the basis for fractions. The apple is one whole piece. How many parts was it sliced into? Each slice is part of the whole apple, or a fraction of it.

4. Language skills. Have your child describe the color and smell of the apple, as well as the reaction of the peanut butter slipping on the apple slice.

Cooking vocabulary to share with your child:

ambrosia: a delectable food or drink

quarter: a part of a whole that is exactly one-fourth

Idea Bags for the Kitchen

Fun activities to do with your child

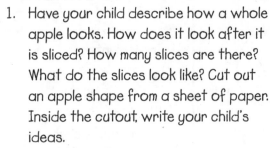

1. Have your child describe how a whole apple looks. How does it look after it is sliced? How many slices are there? What do the slices look like? Cut out an apple shape from a sheet of paper. Inside the cutout, write your child's ideas.

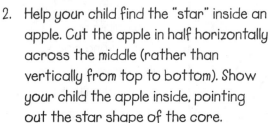

2. Help your child find the "star" inside an apple. Cut the apple in half horizontally across the middle (rather than vertically from top to bottom). Show your child the apple inside, pointing out the star shape of the core.

3. The circumference is the distance around the "waist" of an apple. Using string, help your child measure the circumference of several apples. For each apple, cut the string to show the circumference. Line up the strings for your child to compare. Which string is longer? Which apple, then, is thickest? Let children measure the strings with a ruler and write down the numbers. Help them notice that the bigger numbers correspond with the longer strings.

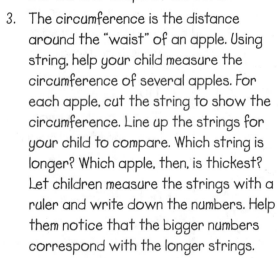

4. If time allows, visit your local library and check out the book *The Seasons of Arnold's Apple Tree* by Gail Gibbons (Voyager Books/Harcourt Brace & Company, 1984). Read it with your child.

Apple Slices and Peanut Butter

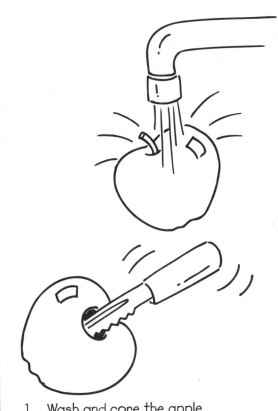
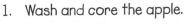

1. Wash and core the apple.

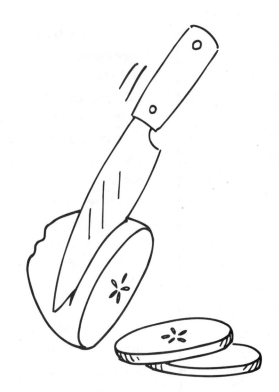

2. Cut the apple into slices.

3. Spread peanut butter on the slice.

4. Eat and enjoy!

Idea Bags for the Kitchen FE11036

Apple Sandwich

Ingredients:
  1/2 cup of cream cheese
  3/4 cup of chopped celery
  3/4 cup of chopped walnuts
  1 cup of chopped apples
  slices of bread

Utensils:
  a cutting board
  a sharp knife (for adult use only)
  measuring cups
  a dull knife

FYI:

The remains of charred apples have been found in the ruins of prehistoric lake dwellings. Stone-Age peoples carved pictures of them.

Tip:

Wrap celery in aluminum foil when storing it in the refrigerator. It will keep for weeks.

Did You Know:

You can bake apples by putting a little water with a touch of sugar in a baking pan. Add a dash of vanilla, then the sliced apples. Bake until soft and tender.

Questions to ask your child while cooking:

1. How many ingredients are we mixing together?
2. Do you think the mixture will be crunchy or smooth?
3. Which ingredient can you taste the most? The least?
4. Which two ingredients were the same amount?
5. On what other foods could you spread the mixture?

Cut along dashed line and glue to a brown paper lunch bag.

4
reproducible

Idea Bags for the Kitchen FE11036

While preparing this recipe, your child is learning:

1. Math skills. Your child is measuring, becoming familiar with part/whole relationships, and adding.

2. Reading skills. Your child is accomplishing a task by reading a sequence of steps with the help of picture clues. Reading pictures in sequence is a first step to reading words. It sharpens concepts of print, such as reading from the left side of the page to the right side.

3. Emotional development. As your child completes the recipe, he or she is learning personal responsibility. Interest, not self-discipline, drives the desire to complete the task. Self-discipline occurs in a later stage of your child's development.

4. Oral-language skills. As your child experiences preparing and eating this dish, he or she becomes familiar with descriptive words, like smooth, bumpy, rough, and crunchy.

Cooking vocabulary to share with your child:

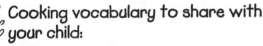

chef: the person responsible for a kitchen cooking team

chop: to cut a food into small pieces

soften: to take a food from the refrigerator or freezer, setting it aside for a while until it thaws a bit and becomes not as solid

Idea Bags for the Kitchen

Fun activities to do with your child

1. Invite your child to taste the nuts, celery, cream cheese, and apple, one at a time. Encourage your child to describe and compare the foods' textures and flavors.

2. Substitute these words for the chant, "Who Took the Cookie from the Cookie Jar?"

You say: Who took the apple from the apple tree? [Insert your child's name] took the apple from the apple tree.

Your child says: Who me?

You say: Yes, you.

Your child says: Couldn't be.

You say: Then who?

Your child then repeats the first two lines, inserting a new name, and the chant continues.

3. Make an apple puzzle. Find or draw a picture of an apple. Cut the picture into as many pieces as you think your child can assemble successfully.

4. Peel a strip of apple skin for your child to taste. Ask your child to compare the outside of the apple with the inside of the apple. How is the texture different? How is the flavor different?

5. Lay two apple slices on a plate. Squeeze some lemon juice on one of them. Have your child observe the changes. (The slice without the lemon juice will begin to turn brown.) Explain that the lemon juice slows the browning process, which occurs when the inside of an apple is exposed to air.

Idea Bags for the Kitchen FE11036

Apple Sandwich

1. Gather the ingredients and utensils.

2. Chop the apple into small pieces until you have 1 cup.

3. Chop the celery into small pieces until you have 3/4 cup.

4. Chop the walnuts into small pieces until you have 3/4 cup.

5. Place the apples, celery, and nuts in a bowl. Add 1/2 cup of cream cheese, too.

6. Mix well.

7. Spread on a slice of bread.

8. Eat and enjoy!

Idea Bags for the Kitchen FE11036

Banana Slices and Raisins

Ingredients:
    1 banana
    1 box of raisins

Utensils:
    a dull knife
    a plate

FYI:

Bananas grow upward in clusters, called "hands." Each hand has 10 to 20 bananas, called "fingers." Each finger is about 5 to 8 inches long.

Tip:

If sliced bananas are going to sit awhile before you use them, sprinkle a little lemon or pineapple juice over them. The juice will keep the bananas from turning brown.

Did You Know:

If you want to mash bananas, you can do so with a potato masher. Let your child try it. Your child will have a ball!

Questions to ask your child while cooking:

1. What words describe the banana with the peel on? Without the peel?

2. What do you see inside each banana slice? What do you think these little dark dots are? (These are the seeds of the banana plant.)

3. How many slices did you cut from your banana?

4. What was the shape of the whole banana? What is the shape of the sliced banana?

5. Is the banana hard? Soft? Crunchy?

6. Are the raisins hard? Soft? Crunchy?

Cut along dashed line and glue to a brown paper lunch bag.

Idea Bags for the Kitchen FE11036

While preparing this recipe, your child is learning:

1. Math skills. Your child is learning part/whole relationships when slicing a whole banana. Your child is also identifying shapes, counting slices and raisins, and matching like quantities.

2. Social skills. Because your child makes several raisin-and-banana snacks, your child is encouraged to share the food with family and friends.

3. Emotional development. Allowing your child to use a dull knife to slice the banana shows your child that you trust him or her to handle the knife responsibly. This, in turn, fosters self-confidence.

4. Science skills. As your child compares raisins and bananas, then raisins and bananas with other fruits, your child is honing the basic science skill of observing similarities and differences. Your child is also encouraged to make predictions, conduct an experiment, then compare predictions with actual results.

Cooking vocabulary to share with your child:

baste: to pour or brush liquid over a food as it cooks, keeping the food moist

beat: to mix vigorously with a beater or a spoon

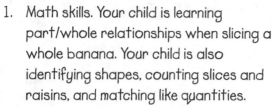

Idea Bags for the Kitchen

Fun activities to do with your child

1. What does your child think will happen to a banana peel if buried for a few months? Try it! First, write down your child's prediction. Then put the banana peel in a sock. Bury the sock, with the open end of the sock sticking from the ground. (This way you will be able to find it.) Check the sock three months later. How has the banana peel changed? Compare what happened with your child's earlier prediction.

2. Make your own raisins from grapes. Talk about the grapes with your child. Compare them with raisins. Point out that grapes have a lot of juice, but raisins do not. How does your child think this happens? Write down your child's ideas. Then place the grapes on a plate, and leave the plate in the sun for several days. The heat from the sun will evaporate the juice, drying the grapes and turning them into raisins.

3. Encourage your child to first compare the physical characteristics of a banana and a raisin, then the physical characteristics of bananas and raisins with other fruits. Challenge your child to identify shapes and colors, as well as to point out which fruits are bigger/smaller than others. Let your child compare textures and flavors, too.

4. Have your child listen closely to the beginning sound of fruit names. Which start with consonants? (For example, banana and raisin.) Which start with vowels? (For example, apple and orange.)

Banana Slices and Raisins

1. Peel the banana.

2. Slice the banana.

3. Put raisins on the banana slices.

4. Eat and enjoy!

Idea Bags for the Kitchen FE11036

Broccoli Bites

Ingredients:
  broccoli florets
  salad dressing

Utensils:
  a plate
  a bowl

FYI:

Broccoli is a cousin of the cauliflower. Broccoli is actually the flowering part of a plant. It is harvested while the flower buds are still tightly closed. If left unharvested, the buds will develop into yellow flowers.

Tip:

When buying broccoli, choose heads that are completely green. The buds on the tips should be tiny, even smaller than a pin head. If the buds are large, or if they are yellow, the broccoli is nearly ready to bloom. In this stage, the broccoli could be tough and not as flavorful.

Questions to ask your child while cooking:

1. Why do you think the flower-like broccoli tips are called florets?
2. How many florets came from the broccoli stalk?
3. How are the broccoli florets like the stem? How are they different?
4. How does broccoli taste different when eaten with salad dressing as compared to when it is eaten without salad dressing?

Cut along dashed line and glue to a brown paper lunch bag.

Idea Bags for the Kitchen FE11036

While preparing this recipe, your child is learning:

1. Reading skills. Your child is expressing ideas with words and recognizing that print and pictures have meaning.

2. Math skills. Your child is exploring part/whole relationships when examining broccoli pieces that have been pulled off a whole broccoli stalk.

3. Science skills. Your child is recognizing and comparing how things are alike and different in the natural world. Your child is also identifying parts of a plant, such as the flowers and the stem.

4. Oral-language skills. Your child will become familiar with words in context, such as floret.

Cooking vocabulary to share with your child:

chiffonnade: vegetables that have been cut into thin, fine strips

chill: to place a food in a refrigerator in order to lower its temperature

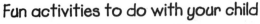

Idea Bags for the Kitchen

Fun activities to do with your child

1. Grow a broccoli garden inside a car tire. Lay the tire flat, and fill the inside with potting soil. Get a package of broccoli seeds, and follow the directions for planting. Allow the broccoli plant to grow from a sprout to an adult. Invite your child to observe how the broccoli buds blossom into flowers.

2. Steam some broccoli. Let your child compare the flavor and texture of the steamed broccoli with raw broccoli. For example, which is easier to chew? How does the color change?

3. Visit your local library and obtain a copy of the book *All Our Fruits and Vegetables* by Roberta Duyff and Patricia McKissack (Many Hands Media, 1995) to share with your child.

4. Set aside a broccoli stem to dry for a day. The stem makes a great printing tool. Spread some newspaper over a table, and give your child a sheet of paper. Pour a small amount of tempera paint into a small dish or jar. Invite your child to dip the broccoli stem into the paint and press the stem to paper to make fun print designs.

Idea Bags for the Kitchen FE11036

Broccoli Bites

1. Wash the broccoli.

2. Pull off the florets.

3. Dip the florets in salad dressing.

4. Eat and enjoy!

Idea Bags for the Kitchen FE11036

Carrot Medallions

Ingredients:

    1 carrot

Utensils:

    a vegetable brush or toothbrush

    a carrot peeler

    a sharp knife (for use by adult only)

FYI:

The word medallion is used to describe any food cut in an oval, or round shape.

Tip:

Let your child use a toothbrush, instead of a vegetable brush, to clean the carrot. A toothbrush is easier for tiny hands to manage when getting at the hard-to-reach surfaces of a carrot.

Questions to ask your child while cooking:

1. Why did we use a brush on the carrot?
2. What were the three tools that helped us cut the carrot into medallions?
3. How many medallions did we make?
4. What color is a carrot? What other foods are this color?
5. What animals do you know that like carrots?

Cut along dashed line and glue to a brown paper lunch bag.

While preparing this recipe, your child is learning:

1. Language skills. New words, like medallion, become part of your child's vocabulary and are used appropriately and in context.

2. Science skills. As your child works with kitchen utensils, your child will begin to understand that tools and simple machines help us do work.

3. Math skills. Your child will identify shapes by recognizing that a medallion is a circle.

4. Writing skills. Your child will be encouraged to write simple noun/verb sentences that identify a kitchen tool and what it does.

Cooking vocabulary to share with your child:

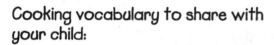

can: a way to preserve food; a container in which food can be kept for a long time

carve: to cut prepared meat or other foods, usually to serve to others

sauté: to cook food in oil over high heat so it slides, but does not stick, in the pan

Idea Bags for the Kitchen

Fun activities to do with your child

1. With your child, look through your kitchen for other foods that when sliced are in the shape of medallions, such as bananas or cucumbers.

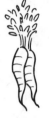

2. Collect a variety of kitchen utensils. Talk with your child about how they are used and how they make kitchen work easier. Encourage your child to draw and label each tool, and to perhaps include a simple sentence to describe it, using proper terminology, such as slice, grate, blend, or peel. For example: A mixer blends.

3. Plant a carrot garden in an aquarium. Fill an empty aquarium with potting soil. Tape some black paper around the outside of the aquarium so the soil is not showing. Then plant carrot seeds, following the directions on the seed packet. Have your child watch the top of the soil and describe the growing plant. Does it look like a carrot? Where might the carrot be growing? When the carrots are fully grown, remove the black paper and examine the carrots below the soil. Explain that the part of a carrot that we eat is actually the root of the carrot plant. It soaks up water and other nutrients from the soil to help the green leafy part grow.

4. Before eating the carrot medallions, place them on a paper plate. Encourage your child to arrange the medallions into simple pictures, such as a face, a car, the sun, a flower. Help your child identify the various shapes he or she creates in the pictures.

Carrot Medallions

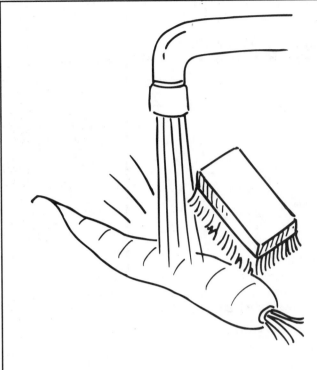

1. Scrub the carrot.

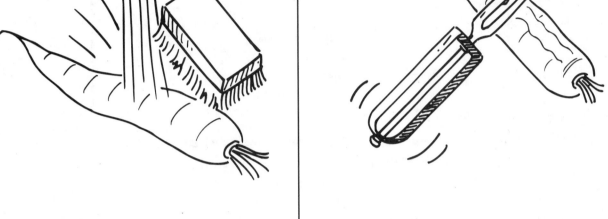

2. Peel the carrot.

3. Slice the carrot.

4. Eat and enjoy!

Idea Bags for the Kitchen FE11036

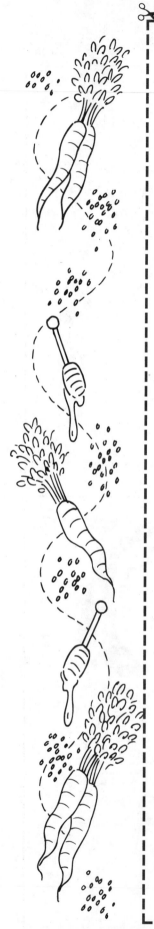

Carrot Honey Sticks

Ingredients:
  1 carrot
  honey
  sesame seeds

Utensils:
  a carrot peeler
  a sharp knife (for adult use only)
  a bowl
  a tray or cookie sheet

FYI:

The wild carrot is called Queen Anne's lace because the green leaves look like lace. They were grown in the Mediterranean region several thousand years ago. In China and in northwestern Europe, carrots were being grown by the 13th century.

Tip:

If honey becomes granulated in its container, place the container in a pan of warm water. The honey will return to liquid form.

Questions to ask your child while cooking:

1. What made the sesame seeds stick to the carrot?
2. Did many seeds or few seeds stick to the carrot? Why?
3. Where do you think carrot seeds are found in the carrot?
4. What other foods have you seen that look like a carrot?
5. What else could you peel with a carrot peeler?
6. When else have you heard the word **sesame**?

Cut along dashed line and glue to a brown paper lunch bag.

While preparing this recipe, your child is learning:

1. Math skills. Your child is comparing quantities and using terms like more than and less than.

2. Reading skills. The words on the recipe page have a repeated pattern: ____ the carrot. Point out to your child the repeated words *the carrot*. Have your child describe the action in the picture, then fill in the new words: Peel the carrot. Slice the carrot. Dip the carrot. Roll the carrot.

3. Science skill. Your child is identifying physical properties, such as hard and soft, solid (carrot) and liquid (honey). Your child is also exploring the things plants need in order to grow, such as soil and water. Your child will also confirm that a carrot is the root part of a plant.

4. Social skills. By slicing the carrot in two, your child is able to share the carrot honey sticks with a friend.

Cooking vocabulary to share with your child:

pastry: a sweet, baked food, usually made from dough

patisserie: the art of making delicious, eye-pleasing pastries, as practiced by a pastry chef; the place where pastries are made and sold

Idea Bags for the Kitchen

Fun activities to do with your child

1. Prepare some cooked carrots, or buy cooked carrots to prepare. Invite your child to taste the cooked carrots, then some raw carrots. Challenge your child to compare the carrots' flavor and texture. Which do they enjoy more-raw carrots or cooked carrots? Why?

2. Review with your child the basic parts of a plant-the root, the stem, the leaves. Ask your child which part of the plant a carrot is. Confirm that it is the root. Share with your child that a radish is also a root. Expose the roots of a house plant for your child to compare with the carrot.

3. Sprout a carrot top on a wet paper towel. In a shallow dish, place several folded-up, moist paper towels. Put the carrot top on top of the towels. Keep the paper towels moist, and observe with your child as the top begins to grow. Remind your child that the carrot is a root, and the root absorbs the water from the paper towels to make the stem and leaves of the plant grow.

4. Place several carrots side by side. Challenge your child to arrange the carrots in order, from shortest to longest. For an extra challenge, have your child arrange them by thinnest to thickest.

Idea Bags for the Kitchen FE11036

Carrot Honey Sticks

1. Gather the ingredients and utensils.

2. Peel the carrot.

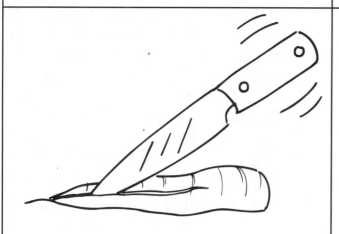

3. Slice the carrot.

4. Dip the carrot in the honey.

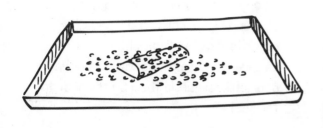

5. Roll the carrot in the sesame seeds.

6. Eat and enjoy!

reproducible

Celery, Peanut Butter, and Raisins

Ingredients:
  celery
  peanut butter
  raisins

Utensils:
  a paper towel
  a dull knife
  a cutting board

FYI:

The life cycle of a celery plant is two years. The stalks are full grown after one year, when they are harvested. The main stem of the celery plant remains behind. It will soon develop into a bushy, seed-bearing plant.

Tip:

If your celery has wilted, place it in a container of ice water. Put the container in the refrigerator. The celery will become crisp in about an hour.

Questions to ask your child while cooking:

1. What noise do you make when you bite into a piece of celery?

2. Is the celery soft or hard? Crunchy or mushy?

3. How many raisins did you put on your peanut-butter-covered celery?

4. What other kind of plant have you seen that looks like a celery stalk?

5. What word would you use to describe the peanut butter?

6. What word would you use to describe the raisins?

Cut along dashed line and glue to a brown paper lunch bag.

Idea Bags for the Kitchen FE11036

While preparing this recipe, your child is learning:

1. Emotional development. As your child works with the dull knife, your child will be experiencing and reinforcing a sense of independence. You are trusting your child to handle the dull knife properly and responsibly. This, in turn, builds self-esteem and self-respect.

2. Language skills. As you talk to your child throughout the activity, you are helping your child sharpen language skills, as well as building vocabulary as your child describes and compares the foods.

3. Math skills. Encourage your child to count the number of raisins as he or she places them on the peanut butter. You could also practice addition and subtraction by asking your child to "add one more" or "take one away," then asking, "How many raisins do you have now?"

4. Science skills. Your child will experiment with a celery stalk, observing as colored water moves through it. Help your child conclude from this experiment that a celery stalk is the stem of a plant that brings water from the plant root to its leaves.

Cooking vocabulary to share with your child:

boil: to heat a liquid until it rolls and bubbles on top, usually reaching a temperature of 212°F (100°C)

broil: to cook a food in the oven, in the area directly under the heating element

Idea Bags for the Kitchen

Fun activities to do with your child

1. Cut apart the recipe pictures. Challenge your child to put the pictures in order to show the correct sequence of the recipe. Invite your child to explain the recipe in order.

2. Share with your child that the celery stalk is actually the stem of a celery plant. The stem brings water and other nutrients in the soil up to the plant leaves. To prove this, fill a glass with water. Add some food coloring. Place a celery stalk in the water. With your child, observe as the colored water is absorbed at the bottom of the stalk and moves upward.

3. Cut a celery stalk in half widthwise. Show your child the celery stalk, and ask what shape it is. (A crescent, the letter C, a crescent moon, for example.) Spread some newspaper over a table, and set out paper and a dish with paint. Let your child dip the celery stalk in the paint, then press it to the paper to make celery prints.

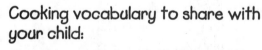

Idea Bags for the Kitchen FE11036

Celery, Peanut Butter, and Raisins

1. Wash the celery.

2. Dry the celery.

3. Slice the celery.

4. Spread peanut butter on the celery.

5. Put raisins on the peanut butter.

6. Eat and enjoy!

Idea Bags for the Kitchen FE11036

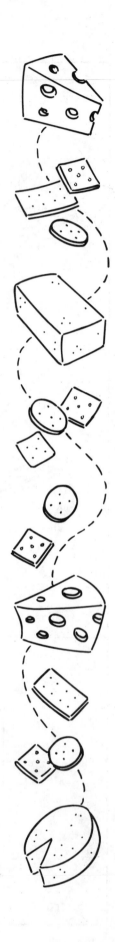

Cheese and Crackers

Ingredients:
- a block of cheese
- crackers

Utensils:
- a dull knife
- a cutting board
- a paper plate

FYI:

Cheese was one of the earliest foods eaten by people. It is made from milk that animals produce. In temperate climates, people make cheese mostly from cow's milk. In mountainous regions, people may make cheese from sheep or goat's milk. In cold climates, cheese can be made from reindeer milk or yak milk. And in Africa, they even make cheese from zebra milk!

Tip:

To keep cheese fresh and moist, wrap it in a cloth dampened with vinegar. Store the cloth-wrapped cheese in an airtight container.

Did You Know:

You can rub butter or margarine over the end of the cheese that has been cut to prevent it from drying out.

Questions to ask your child while cooking:

1. Was the cheese hard or soft? Was it easy or difficult to cut?
2. If you put cheese between two crackers, could you call it a cheese-and-cracker sandwich? Why?
3. How are the cheese and the crackers different?
4. How would you compare the color of the cheese to the color of the cracker?

Cut along dashed line and glue to a brown paper lunch bag.

reproducible

Idea Bags for the Kitchen FE11036

While preparing this recipe, your child is learning:

1. Math skills. Ask your child to cut a slice of cheese for each cracker. Have your child put the cheese and crackers together. If there are leftover crackers or slices of cheese, encourage your child to point out which has more—the cheese or the crackers.

2. Social skills. The recipe page encourages your child to share the cheese-and-cracker snacks with a friend.

3. Oral-language skills. As your child shares the cheese and crackers with a friend, your child may feel compelled to explain how the snack was prepared, strengthening oral language.

4. Science skills. When your child learns about other dairy products, he or she is sharpening comparing and grouping skills, as well as learning about one of the food groups.

Cooking vocabulary to share with your child:

connoisseur: a person who is especially competent to judge the art of cooking

coq: the name of the chef aboard a ship

Idea Bags for the Kitchen

Fun activities to do with your child

1. Set a variety of cheeses on a plate. Invite your child to sample the various cheeses, describing their flavors. Ask your child which cheese he or she likes the most, and encourage your child to explain why.

2. Next to the block of cheese, place a carton of milk. You might also set out a carton of yogurt, ice cream, cottage cheese, or butter. Ask your child what these foods have in common. Explain that they are all dairy products, which means that each product was made from milk.

3. Find a magazine photo or draw a picture of a block of cheese. (You could also invite your child to do it.) Cut the picture apart into shapes your child can handle. Mix up the shapes, and challenge your child to put the cheese puzzle together.

4. Invite your child to create a cheese still-life painting. Have fun with your child setting up the cheese "model." For example, you might choose a colorful plate to set the cheese on, create a fun background with flowers or fruits, or place a stuffed animal beside the cheese to represent an animal eating it. Give your child paper and pencil, and invite him or her to draw the scene. Let your child erase and fix the picture as desired. Then supply paints, and encourage your child to add in the colors to bring the still-life to "life."

Idea Bags for the Kitchen FE11036

Cheese and Crackers

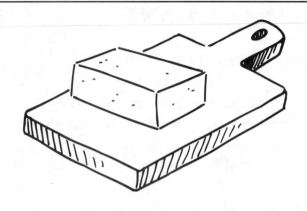

1. Put the cheese on a cutting board.

2. Slice the cheese.

3. Put the crackers on a plate.

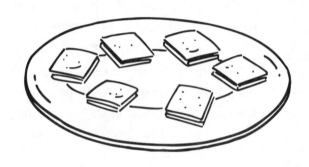

4. Put the cheese on the crackers.

5. Share the cheese and crackers with a friend.

6. Eat and enjoy!

Idea Bags for the Kitchen FE11036

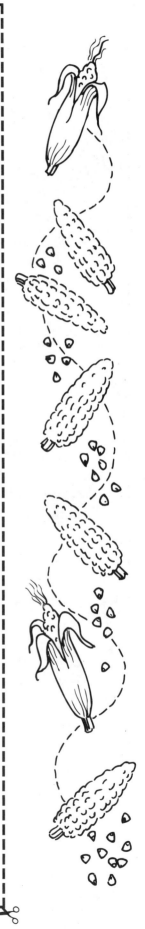

Corn on the Cob

Ingredients:

ears of corn   boiling water

butter

Utensils:

a large pot   a stove burner

tongs   a plate   a timer

FYI:

Native Americans who lived in central and southern Mexico gathered and ate corn 10,000 years ago. The corn was actually gathered from wild plants that grew in the area. In fact, fossils of corncobs have been found, dating back 7,000 years. These ancient corncobs were 1 inch long and had about 50 to 60 kernels each.

Tip:

To avoid the corn from becoming tough, salt it halfway through the boiling process. You can also add a dash of sugar to make the corn more flavorful.

Did You Know:

Vegetables grown above ground, like corn, are boiled without a lid. Vegetables grown below the ground, like carrots, are boiled with a lid.

Questions to ask your child while cooking:

1. What do you think will happen to the corn when it is put in the boiling water and cooked for 15 minutes?

2. What else can you think of that takes 15 minutes to do? What could you do while the corn is cooking?

3. Feel the air above the boiling water. Is it warm or cool? Why is it warm?

4. How many kernels do you estimate are on one ear of corn? Do you think each ear of corn has the same number of kernels? Why or why not?

Cut along dashed line and glue to a brown paper lunch bag.

While preparing this recipe, your child is learning:

1. Math skills. Your child can estimate the number of corn kernels in one row, then count the kernels to find the actual number. Your child is also learning time awareness while waiting for the corn to cook. Your child can also compare sizes of corncobs and corn kernels.

2. Science skills. Watching food boil demonstrates the three states of matter: the water is a liquid; the corn is a solid; and the steam from the boiling water is a gas. Your child also notices how heat changes something (causing the water to boil), how the boiling water changes the corn, and how warm corn will melt butter.

3. Safety issues. While the water is boiling, you will reinforce with your child that he or she should not touch the stove burner, the pot, or the water because they are hot and dangerous.

4. Social studies skills. If you are able to visit a local farm to pick husks of corn, your child will learn that people in the community provide us with things we need, like food.

Cooking vocabulary to share with your child:

grease: to rub the surface of cooking utensils, such as cookie sheets or frying pans, with shortening or butter so the food will not stick while cooking

Idea Bags for the Kitchen

Fun activities to do with your child

1. Before cooking the corn, challenge your child to arrange the ears of corn in order of size, from shortest to longest.

2. If the corn still has its green leafy covering, invite your child to help shuck the corn. With clean hands, let your child feel the texture of the corn and describe it. You could also count the number of leaves pulled from the corn as you shuck them.

3. After eating the corn, set aside the empty corncobs to dry. Slice one dried corncob into small disks. Invite your child to use the disks to create a collage on sturdy paper or on a paper plate, by gluing the disks in place.

4. Use the remaining dried corncobs to create corn prints. Cover a table with newspaper, and pour some paint into shallow dishes. Give your child art paper and the dried corncobs. Let your child dip the cobs into the paint and roll them on paper.

5. If possible, visit the cornfield of a local farmer. Invite your child to have fun picking ears of corn with you. You might ask the farmer to provide a demonstration to make sure the corn is picked correctly.

Idea Bags for the Kitchen FE11036

Corn on the Cob

1. Put a large pot of water on the stove to boil.

2. Shuck the corn.

3. Put the corn in boiling water.

4. Cook the corn for 15 minutes.

5. Turn off the heat. Lift the corn from the water with tongs.

6. Put the corn on a plate to cool.

7. Spread butter over the corn.

8. Eat and enjoy!

Idea Bags for the Kitchen FE11036

Roasted Corn

Ingredients:
    3 to 4 ears of corn
    margarine or butter
    salt and pepper

Utensils:
    foil
    oven
    a plate

FYI:

Corn has been eaten for thousands of years. It has been boiled, roasted, baked, steamed, creamed, and popped. Corn is especially rich in starch, fats, and proteins, but not in amino acids, which are essential for a balanced diet.

Tip:

It is best to roast 3 to 4 ears of corn at a time to get the most even cooking. Seal the aluminum foil carefully so liquid will not leak into the oven.

Questions to ask your child while cooking:

1. Why do you think it is important to wrap the corn in foil before roasting?

2. How many pieces of corn, or kernels, do you estimate are on each ear? How could you find out for sure?

3. In summer, on a very hot day, the temperature may reach 100°F. How hot, then, is 400°F?

4. Do you think the 25 minutes passed by slowly or quickly? What did we do during that 25 minutes?

5. What other activity could take us 25 minutes to do?

Cut along dashed line and glue to a brown paper lunch bag.

While preparing this recipe, your child is learning:

1. Math skills. Counting, measuring, estimating, and timing are practiced and sharpened as your child enjoys this recipe and the activities.

2. Language skills. Introducing and using the new word **roasted** improves and strengthens your child's language and vocabulary.

3. Science skills. Your child will have an increased awareness of the five senses as your child views and tastes the corn, salt, pepper, and butter and recognizes how they differ.

4. Creative-thinking skills. By encouraging your child to come up with creative ways to use the empty corncobs, you are sharpening your child's creative-thinking skills.

Cooking vocabulary to share with your child:

menu: a written list of food and drink that is served in a restaurant

mill: a small machine used to grind or crush certain foods, like pepper

Idea Bags for the Kitchen

Fun activities to do with your child

1. Before cooking the ears of corn, help your child measure their lengths, as well as their circumferences. Write down each number. Challenge your child to rewrite the numbers in order, from smallest to largest. Then have your child match the ears of corn with their measurements.

2. Visit your local library, and check out the book *Corn Is Maize* by Aliki (Harpercollins, 1996). Read the book with your child.

3. Rinse and save the corncobs. Let them dry for a few days. Then speculate with your child what you could do with the now-empty cobs. Brainstorm various ideas with your child. Then select one idea to put into action.

4. Share with your child that corn can be made into flour and used to make bread products. With your child, visit the local grocery, and look for such items as corn tortillas and corn bread. If possible, purchase these foods to try at home. Ask your child to compare their flavors with the flavor of the roasted corn. How are they the same? How are they different? Why might they be different? Remind your child that other ingredients have been added to these foods, which might change the flavor slightly.

Roasted Corn

1. Rub butter on the corn.

2. Sprinkle salt and pepper on the corn.

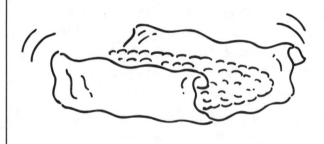

3. Wrap the corn in foil.

4. Put the corn in the oven at 400°F.

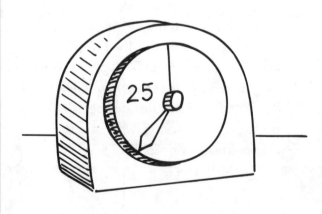

5. Set a timer for 25 minutes. Roast the corn for 25 minutes.

6. Eat and enjoy!

Idea Bags for the Kitchen FE11036

Fruit Drink

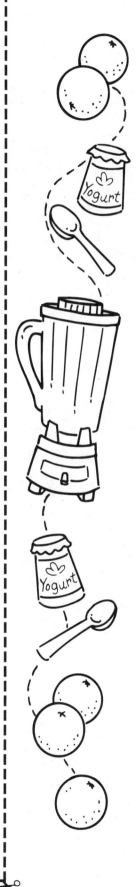

Ingredients:

1 cup of orange juice   1 cup of yogurt

1 teaspoon of vanilla   ice cubes

Utensils:

a blender   a measuring cup

a teaspoon   a glass

FYI:

Yogurt has been eaten in Iran, Turkey, and other Middle Eastern countries for thousands of years. A dairy food, yogurt has been linked to myth and folklore. It has been used to cure insomnia, to remove wrinkles, and to recapture youth.

Tip:

To clean a blender, half fill it with water and add one drop of liquid soap. Put on the lid, and turn on the blender for a few seconds. Be sure to then rinse it clean.

Did You Know:

You can grease the inside of your blender by spraying it with nonstick vegetable spray.

Questions to ask your child while cooking:

1. What were the three ingredients we put in the blender, in order?
2. How did the liquid change when each ingredient was added?
3. What do you like most about the fruit drink? What do you like least?
4. How are orange juice and yogurt alike? How are they different?
5. Suppose you didn't use a blender. How would the drink change if the ingredients were mixed with a spoon? A whisk? A fork?

Cut along dashed line and glue to a brown paper lunch bag.

While preparing this recipe, your child is learning:

1. Reading skills. As your child puts the recipe pictures in order, your child is recalling and retelling events in sequence. Your child can also recognize and read the repeated word *pour* in the directions.

2. Science skills. As the drink is being made, your child is observing change and cause and effect. With the aid of the blender, your child is also learning that tools make work easier. For example, would it be harder or easier to stir the drink with a finger, rather than with a spoon or a blender?

3. Math skills. Measuring ingredients sharpens math skills.

4. Self awareness. As your child evaluates the drink for flavor, he or she is expressing opinions.

Cooking vocabulary to share with your child:

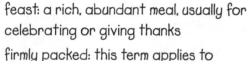

feast: a rich, abundant meal, usually for celebrating or giving thanks

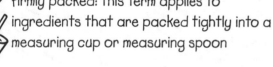

firmly packed: this term applies to ingredients that are packed tightly into a measuring cup or measuring spoon

Idea Bags for the Kitchen

Fun activities to do with your child

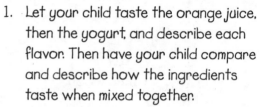

1. Let your child taste the orange juice, then the yogurt, and describe each flavor. Then have your child compare and describe how the ingredients taste when mixed together.

2. Experiment mixing the ingredients with different utensils, such as a fork, a spoon, a whisk, even your finger. Encourage your child to notice which utensils make the job easier.

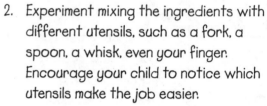

3. Invite your child to suggest other fruit juices to substitute for the orange juice. Mix up a new batch of fruit drink and ask your child to taste and compare the tastes.

4. Cut apart the recipe. Mix up the pictures. Challenge your child to put the pictures in order to show the correct sequence for making the fruit drink.

5. Tape-record a number of kitchen appliances in use, such as a blender, a microwave, a toaster, an eggbeater, a can opener. Play the tape for your child, and challenge your child to identify the sounds.

Idea Bags for the Kitchen FE11036

Fruit Drink

1. Set up the blender.

2. Pour in 1 cup of orange juice.

3. Pour in 1 cup of yogurt.

4. Pour in 1 teaspoon of vanilla.

5. Turn the blender on high.

6. Put ice cubes in a glass.

7. Pour fruit drink into glass.

8. Drink and enjoy!

Idea Bags for the Kitchen FE11036

Grape Pops

Ingredients:
   grape juice

Utensils:
   an ice-cube tray
   Popsicle sticks
   sheet of aluminum foil

FYI:

Scientists believe that grapes have been around for millions of years. That's because fossilized grape leaves, seeds, and stems have been found throughout the Northern Hemisphere, some dating back perhaps 40 million years. The cultivation of grapes appears in paintings on ancient Egyptian tombs, dating back to 2440 B.C.E.

Did You Know:

If grape juice stains your hands, you can wipe them with a slice of raw potato, then wash. You can also use lemon juice, vinegar, or a mixture of salt and lemon juice.

Questions to ask your child while cooking:

1. What do you think will happen to the grape juice in the freezer?

2. Will the grape juice change? How?

3. How could you turn the frozen grape juice back into a liquid?

4. How many grape pops did we make?

5. How is grape juice like a grape?

Cut along dashed line and glue to a brown paper lunch bag.

Idea Bags for the Kitchen FE11036

While preparing this recipe, your child is learning:

1. Science skills. Watching a liquid change into a solid through freezing, and a solid change into a liquid by melting, helps your child understand cause-and-effect relationships. It also introduces the idea that an object can exist in different states—as a solid, a liquid, or a gas. Your child will also experiment with blending colors to create new colors.

2. Reading skills. When your child guesses what could happen to the grape juice inside the freezer, he or she is practicing making predictions, an important aspect of reading comprehension.

3. Math skills. Your child will reinforce number skills when counting the compartments in an ice-cube tray, then counting out a matching number of Popsicle sticks. You can also encourage your child to count by 2's, or to double one row of compartments to get a total number.

4. Social skills. Because many grape pops are made at once, your child can share the pops with friends and family.

Cooking vocabulary to share with your child:

manier: a French term for working a mixture by hand

melt: to warm up a solid until it becomes a liquid

Idea Bags for the Kitchen

Fun activities to do with your child

1. Let your child choose different juices from which to make frozen pops in the same way. Have your child compare the colors of the pops, as well as the flavors.

2. Partially fill two half-gallon milk containers with water. Add some red food coloring to one container, and add some blue food coloring to the other. Set the containers in the freezer until nearly frozen. Then dump the frozen blocks of colored water into a large bowl so they sit side by side. Have your child identify each color, then ask your child to predict what color the water will become when the two blocks begin to melt. (The water should turn purple.) After observing what happens, have your child compare the color to the color of the grape juice.

3. Invite your child to eat some grapes, then to sample some grape juice. Have your child compare the flavors, then suggest ways that the juice from the grape could have been made into grape juice. You might read the ingredients on the grape-juice bottle to point out other ingredients that were added.

4. Make the frozen grape-juice cubes without the Popsicle sticks. Put them in a glass for your child to observe. Have your child predict what will happen, then check the prediction. Let your child drink the melted juice.

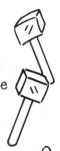

Grape Pops

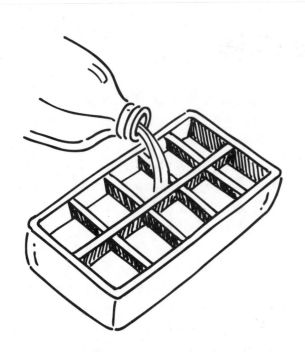

1. Pour grape juice into an ice-cube tray.

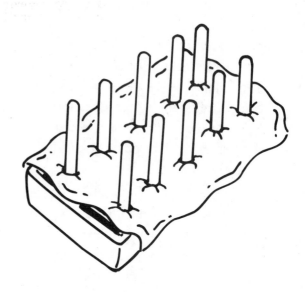

2. Cover tray with aluminum foil. Put sticks inside each section.

3. Put the ice-cube tray in the freezer.

4. Wait until frozen. Eat and enjoy!

Idea Bags for the Kitchen FE11036

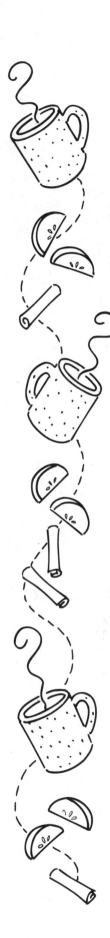

Hot Apple Cider

Ingredients:

  1 cup of apple juice

  1 tablespoon of orange-juice concentrate

  1 cinnamon stick

Utensils:

  a stove burner

  measuring spoons

  a measuring cup

  a mug

FYI:

Apple cider is made from the juice of washed apples. The apples are ground into a fine pulp, called pomace. The pomace is taken to a cider press, where it is placed between a series of cloth layers. The juice is then extracted under pressure.

Questions to ask your child while cooking:

1. How is the flavor of apple cider similar to the flavor of an apple? How is it different?

2. Why do you think this recipe suggests that the apple cider be warm?

3. What other way could you enjoy apple cider? (Cold, for example.)

4. Do you think you could use other fruit to make cider? Which fruit might be tasty as hot cider?

5. How many apples do you think it takes to make one glass of apple juice?

6. Change this recipe to grape cider. What would you put in it?

Cut along dashed line and glue to a brown paper lunch bag.

While preparing this recipe, your child is learning:

1. Science skills. As your child prepares the cider with you, your child is observing the interaction of various ingredients and how they can change. Your child is also observing and learning how heat can change a substance.

2. Creative-thinking skills. Your child will think creatively while making up a story about an apple that becomes apple cider, as well as recalling various apple dishes and suggesting new ones.

3. Math skills. As your child measures ingredients, he or she is recognizing numbers on a measuring cup and counting quantity. Your child is also learning increments of time, such as 5 minutes.

4. Reading Skills. As your child reads the recipe directions, your child is recognizing basic concepts of print. For example, a sentence starts with a word that has a beginning capital letter and ends with a period or an exclamation point.

Cooking vocabulary to share with your child:

finger bowl: a small bowl of water, usually with a slice of lemon, in which fingers can be dipped and cleaned

comb: a tool used to rake crumbs from the table between the courses of a meal

Idea Bags for the Kitchen

Fun activities to do with your child

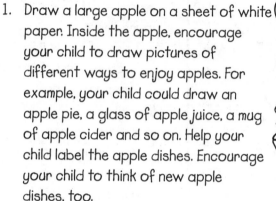

1. Draw a large apple on a sheet of white paper. Inside the apple, encourage your child to draw pictures of different ways to enjoy apples. For example, your child could draw an apple pie, a glass of apple juice, a mug of apple cider and so on. Help your child label the apple dishes. Encourage your child to think of new apple dishes, too.

2. Pour a glass of apple juice. Invite your child to compare the apple juice with the hot apple cider. Speculate with your child which drink would be nicer on a hot summer day. Which would taste better on a cold winter day?

3. Visit your local library to obtain a copy of the book *Rain Makes Applesauce* by Julian Scheer and Marvin Bileck (Holiday House, 1976). Read the book with your child. Ask your child to summarize how rain makes applesauce.

4. Visit the fruit section of your local grocery store with your child. Point out the many varieties of apples. Invite your child to describe and compare them. For example, those apples are bigger than those. Those apples are red, those are green, those are red and green, and those are yellow.

5. Encourage your child to make up a story about an apple that becomes apple cider.

Hot Apple Cider

1. Gather the ingredients and the cooking tools.

2. Pour the apple juice in the pot.

3. Put the orange-juice concentrate in the pot.

4. Put the cinnamon stick in the pot.

5. Heat the ingredients until boiling.

6. Reduce heat. Simmer for 5 minutes.

7. Pour the hot apple cider into a mug. Wait until it cools a bit.

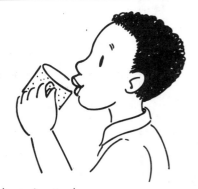

8. Drink and enjoy!

Idea Bags for the Kitchen FE11036

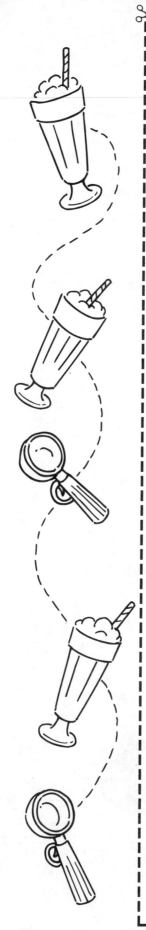

Milk Shake

Ingredients:
   1 cup of milk   2 scoops of ice cream

Utensils:
   a measuring cup
   an ice-cream scooper
   a blender
   a glass

FYI:

Historians indicate that ice cream was brought to North America by the early English colonists. They made ice cream in their homes using metal bowls cooled with ice and salt. (Ice and salt together lower temperature more than ice alone.)

Tip:

If you do not have a blender, you can mix the ingredients by hand.

Did You Know:

You can put foil over the ice cream inside an ice-cream container. This will stop ice crystals from forming on top. Tuck the foil as tightly as possible.

Questions to ask your child while cooking:

1. What noise does the blender make while working?
2. What happened to the ingredients when you turned on the blender? How did they change?
3. How is a milk shake different from a glass of milk?
4. What other flavors of ice cream would you like to use?
5. How did the measuring tools help you make the milk shake?
6. Could you use a scooper to measure the milk? Why or why not?

Cut along dashed line and glue to a brown paper lunch bag.

Idea Bags for the Kitchen FE11036

While preparing this recipe, your child is learning:

1. Science skills. Your child can identify the liquid milk and the solid ice cream, then observe how the blender combines and changes them.

2. Writing skills. Your child is strengthening writing skills and an understanding for sentence construction when copying the recipe and inserting a favorite ice-cream flavor.

3. Math skills. Encourage your child to say the numbers out loud and point to them on the recipe page for each stage of the cooking process. For example, 1 cup of milk; 2 scoops of ice cream. This will reinforce number recognition.

4. Reading skills. When your child follows the cooking directions, your child becomes aware of the relationship between printed words and meaning.

Cooking vocabulary to share with your child:

blend: to gently mix ingredients until smooth

freeze: to place a food in the freezer until it is frozen

Idea Bags for the Kitchen

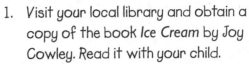

Fun activities to do with your child

1. Visit your local library and obtain a copy of the book *Ice Cream* by Joy Cowley. Read it with your child.

2. If possible, try to obtain an ice-cream-making machine. Many modern ones are available. Or, someone you know might have an old-fashioned hand-cranked machine. Follow the directions with your child to make your own homemade ice cream.

3. Encourage your child to recall and retell the milk-shake-making process. Ask your child to choose a favorite ice cream. Write the word for the ice-cream flavor on a sheet of paper. Then help your child rewrite the recipe, inserting the name of the ice cream. Suggest that your child write each step on a separate sheet of paper. Have your child illustrate the steps, too. Then combine the pages, and let your child create a cover with the title, "My Milk Shake Book." Share the book with family and friends.

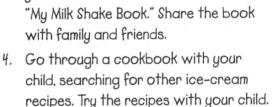

4. Go through a cookbook with your child, searching for other ice-cream recipes. Try the recipes with your child.

5. If possible, locate an ice-cream shop that makes its own ice cream. Call ahead to see if your child can watch the ice-cream-making process.

Milk Shake

1. Pour 1 cup of milk into a blender.

2. Add 2 scoops of ice cream.

3. Put the lid on the blender.

4. Turn the blender on high.

5. Turn off the blender. Pour the milk shake into a glass.

6. Drink and enjoy!

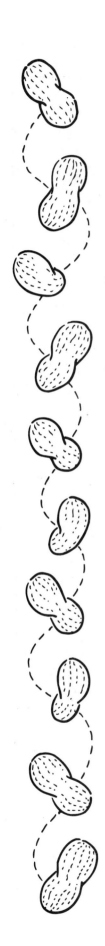
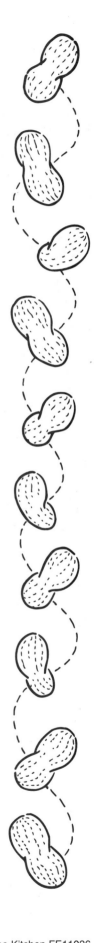

Shelling Peanuts

Ingredients:
    roasted peanuts, still in their shells

Utensils:
    a bowl
    a bigger bowl or pan
    a plate

FYI:

George Washington Carver, an African American scientist, invented over 300 uses for the peanut. Besides being a high-protein, nutritious food, oil from peanuts can be used in soap, facial powders, shaving cream, shampoo, and paint.

Tip:

To better manage clean up, have children shell their peanuts over a large, deep-sided tray or pan. Place the bowl of unshelled peanuts in the center of the pan. Have children drop the empty shells in the pan as they remove the shells from the peanuts.

Questions to ask your child while cooking:

1. How many peanuts are generally in one peanut shell?
2. How does the peanut shell resemble the peanuts inside?
3. What happens to the peanut shell when you squeeze it?
4. What could you do with the empty peanut shell?
5. How are the peanuts like peanut butter?

Cut along dashed line and glue to a brown paper lunch bag.

While preparing this recipe, your child is learning:

1. Fine-motor skills. Using hands and fingers to break open the shells strengthens your child's small muscles and muscle dexterity.

2. Language skills. As your child shells the peanuts, your child becomes familiar with position words. For example: Peanuts are inside the shells. Let's take the peanuts out of the shells. The empty shells are around the peanut bowl. The bowl is sitting in the pan.

3. Writing skills. As your child describes a peanut and writes down the words, your child will be practicing and honing writing skills.

4. Math skills. The peanuts make wonderful sorting, counting, adding, subtracting, and estimating tools. Your child can also measure peanuts and compare the size, weight, and volume of shelled and unshelled peanuts.

Cooking vocabulary to share with your child:

cut-in: to mix shortening with dry ingredients using two knives

datois: tiny snacks

Idea Bags for the Kitchen

Fun activities to do with your child

1. Ask your child to count how many unshelled peanuts she or he can hold in one hand. Let your child write the number. Have your child shell the peanuts, then count how many shelled nuts she or he can hold in the same hand. Have your child write this number, too. Compare the numbers to determine which type of peanut was easier to hold. Why might this be?

2. Put a handful of unshelled peanuts in a jar. Encourage your child to estimate how many peanuts are in the jar, then help your child count the peanuts. Repeat the activity with shelled peanuts.

3. Draw a peanut shell on a large sheet of drawing paper. Ask your child to identify the food you've drawn. Then brainstorm with your child words to describe a peanut shell and the peanut inside. Words can describe shape, color, texture, odor, even taste. Write down your child's words within the peanut-shell shape.

4. In a bowl, mix unshelled peanuts with empty peanut shells and shelled peanuts. Set up three smaller bowls. Challenge your child to sort the mix into shelled peanuts, empty shells, and full shells. Have your child place each type in a different bowl.

Shelling Peanuts

1. Put a bowl of peanuts in a big pan.

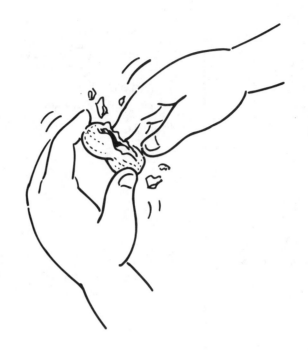

2. Crack open the peanut shell.

3. Put the peanut on a plate. Put the shell in the pan.

4. Share the peanuts with a friend. Eat and enjoy!

Idea Bags for the Kitchen FE11036

Cracking Nuts

Ingredients:
   a variety of edible nuts

Utensils:
   a nutcracker
   a plate
   a bowl

FYI:

Botanists define a nut as a fruit with one or two seeds in a hard shell that does not open on its own. If left in the ground, the shell will rot away, leaving the nut to sprout under the right growing conditions. Many edible nuts, like hazelnuts, pecans, and walnuts, are true nuts, while other nuts, like almonds and coconuts, are not. Twenty-five varieties of nuts are raised as crops.

Did you know:

You can shell pecans and walnuts more easily if you soak them overnight in salt water.

Questions to ask your child while cooking:

1. How are all the nuts alike? How are they different?

2. What other tools, besides a nutcracker, could you use to break open the shell and remove the nut?

3. Why do you think the shell is so hard?

4. What other words could describe the shells?

5. Which nut did you like best? Which nut did you like least?

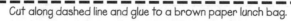

Cut along dashed line and glue to a brown paper lunch bag.

While preparing this recipe, your child is learning:

1. Science skills. Using the nutcracker, your child will discover that this tool is an example of a simple machine-the lever. The nutcracker makes work easier. Your child will also learn that a nut is often the seed part of a plant from which a new plant can grow.

2. Math skills. Your child can practice simple addition and subtraction skills by manipulating the nuts. Comparing nuts for size, weight, shape, and color also reinforces early math skills. Tallying votes to determine the most popular nut sharpens counting, comparison, and number recognition skills.

3. Oral-language skills. As your child compares and describes nuts, expresses his or her own preferences, and asks family members and friends to choose their favorite nuts, your child is practicing oral-language skills.

4. Writing skills. Labeling pictures of nuts will help your child make the connection between the word and the object, as well as provide practice for writing letters.

Cooking vocabulary to share with your child:

dice: to cut food into small pieces of approximately the same size and shape

Idea Bags for the Kitchen

Fun activities to do with your child

1. Provide your child with a variety of nutcrackers. Let your child experiment with them. Which nutcracker does your child find easiest to use? Along with traditional, store-bought nutcrackers, let your child crack the nuts with a small hammer, a rock, and so on.

2. Encourage your child to sort the nuts by size, shape, and color.

3. Let your child count the nuts and write the total number. Take away some of the nuts, and ask your child how many are left. Add more nuts, and ask how many nuts there are now. Have your child pose such "nut problems" to you, too.

4. On a small kitchen scale, have your child weigh one nut. Write down its weight. Challenge your child to choose a nut that could weigh the same. Weigh it as well. Compare the weights to see which weighs more.

5. On large paper, have your child draw the various nuts, both with and without their shells. Help your child label each nut. Ask your child to circle the nut he or she likes the most.

6. Invite your child to take a survey of friends and family to determine which nut is most popular. Help your child draw tally marks for each vote, then add up the tallies to find the winner.

Cracking Nuts

1. Put some nuts on a plate.

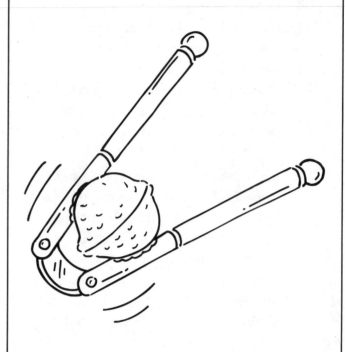

2. Choose one nut. Crack it open with the nutcracker.

3. Take out the insides. Put the shells in a bowl.

4. Eat and enjoy!

Idea Bags for the Kitchen FE11036

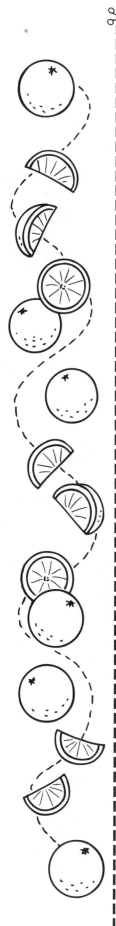

Orange Slices

Ingredients:
  1 orange

Utensils:
  a plate
  a sharp knife (for use by adult only)

FYI:

People have been growing oranges for more than 4,000 years. Oranges first appeared in Asia. Arab traders then introduced oranges to Africa and the Middle East. Columbus brought the first orange seeds to America in 1493.

Tip:

To more easily peel the orange skin from the pulpy fruit, put the orange in hot water for five minutes before peeling.

Questions to ask your child while cooking:

1. What happens when you cut through the orange skin and into the fruit itself?

2. Where do you think the juice comes from that squirts from the cut you make?

3. What shape are the sections of a peeled orange?

4. What other fruit can you think of have sections inside?

5. How many oranges slices did we cut?

Cut along dashed line and glue to a brown paper lunch bag.

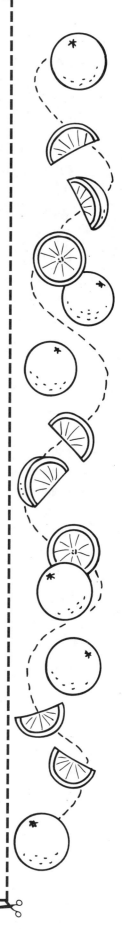

Idea Bags for the Kitchen FE11036

While preparing this recipe, your child is learning:

1. Science skills. As your child recognizes the triangular patterns of the orange sections, you are reinforcing that nature has patterns. You can also reinforce the fact that seeds found in a fruit will grow a new plant.

2. Math skills. As children compare the weights of apples and oranges, they'll be connecting numbers with real-world activities. Your child will also learn about fractions as the orange is cut first into halves, then into quarters.

3. Safety skills. Stress to your child that kitchen knives are for preparing foods. They need to be handled properly and responsibly. If they are not, people can get hurt.

4. Self awareness. As your child tastes different types of oranges, he or she will express opinions and preferences.

Cooking vocabulary to share with your child:

bake: to cook a food in an oven

shred: to cut a food into thin strips, often using a tool called a shredder

zest: the exterior skin of an orange, lemon, or other citrus fruit

Idea Bags for the Kitchen

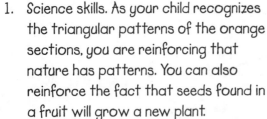

Fun activities to do with your child

1. On a kitchen scale, invite your child to weigh an orange. Write down the weight. Then ask your child to weigh an apple. Write down its weight, too. With your child, compare the numbers. Which fruit weighs more? How can they tell? (The number will be higher or bigger.) If you have a balance scale, place one fruit on each side. The heavier fruit will sit lower than the lighter fruit.

2. If your orange had seeds, save them for your child to grow. Place them on a paper towel to dry overnight. Fold another paper towel so it will fit inside a plastic baggie. Wet the towel, slip it inside the baggie, then place the seeds on top of the wet towel. Seal the baggie. Invite your child to observe over the next few days as the seeds begin to sprout. Remind your child that the seeds for a plant can be found inside the plant's fruit.

3. Share with your child a variety of oranges. Tell your child the name of each orange, too. Have your child compare the flavor and texture of each orange, and let your child decide which orange is his or her favorite.

4. Invite your child to think of another way to eat an orange. For example, would your child like the orange with yogurt? Ice cream? Cottage cheese? Follow your child's suggestion to create a new orange treat.

Orange Slices

1. Slice an orange in half.

2. Slice each orange half in half again.

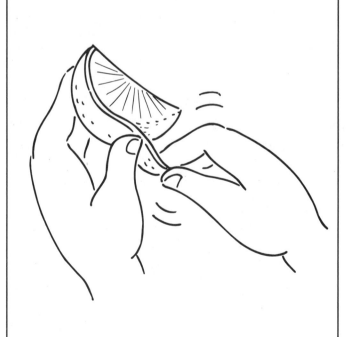

3. Peel the orange slice.

4. Eat and enjoy!

Idea Bags for the Kitchen FE11036

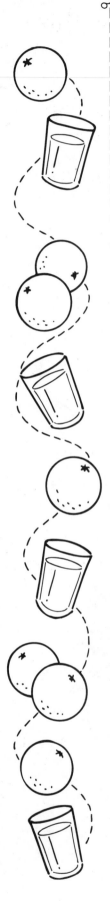

Orange Juice

Ingredients:

1 orange   ice cubes

Utensils:

a plate

a sharp knife (for use by adult only)

a juicer

a glass

FYI:

Before World War II, nearly all orange juice was marketed as "fresh juice." In 1944, however, scientists found a way to concentrate the juice. Frozen, concentrated orange juice become widely popular. Today, 70% of the annual orange crop in the United States is used to make orange-juice concentrate.

Tip:

Instead of throwing the orange peels away, wash and save them. Let your child drop the peels into a glass of water. This will give the water an orange flavor.

Did You Know:

You can freeze fresh orange juice into ice-cube trays. Drop the frozen cubes into water or orange juice for a refreshing juice drink.

Questions to ask your child while cooking:

1. What words describe an orange? What does the orange peel look like? What does it feel like?
2. How is an orange like an apple? How is it different?
3. Where does orange juice come from?
4. What does the inside of the orange look like? How does it compare to the outside?
5. How much juice do you think you could get from this one orange?

Cut along dashed line and glue to a brown paper lunch bag.

While preparing this recipe, your child is learning:

1. Reading skills. Your child can become familiar with the letter **o**, for it is the same shape as an orange, which begins with the letter **o**.

2. Math skills. When your child cuts an orange in half, your child is being introduced to fractions. For example, 2 half oranges (1/2 + 1/2) equal 1 whole orange. Your child reinforces number recognition and understanding bigger and smaller numbers by measuring and weighing oranges and comparing the results. Your child also hones sorting and grouping skills by separating citrus fruits into like groups.

3. Science skills. As your child studies the inside of the oranges, your child will recognize the triangular pattern, fostering an understanding of the patterns found in nature. If the orange has seeds, the activity reinforces that the fruit of a plant holds the seeds.

4. Geography skills. Oranges mainly grow in warm areas. Share with your child if oranges are grown in your area. Point out northern and southern areas on a map.

Cooking vocabulary to share with your child:

banquet: a large meal, often festive, that is eaten along with others

flour: to sprinkle a food lightly with flour

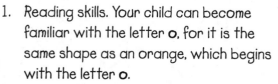

Idea Bags for the Kitchen

Fun activities to do with your child

1. Set up seven oranges on a table. Ask your child to count how many oranges there are. You might write the number 7 so your child can associate the printed number with the actual amount. Then ask your child to arrange the oranges in order of size, from smallest to largest.

2. Create a pile of various citrus fruits, such as grapefruits, oranges, limes, lemons, and tangerines. Challenge your child to sort the fruits into like groups. Help your child identify each fruit, too.

3. Use the juicer to make other fruit juices, such as lemon juice and grapefruit juice. Invite your child to compare the flavors of these juices with the orange juice.

4. Using a tape measure, help your child measure the circumference of several oranges. Write down the numbers. Have your child compare the numbers to determine which orange is thickest.

5. Weigh different oranges as well, and write down the weights. Talk about the different weights. Let your child weigh other citrus fruits, too. Which fruits are the heaviest? The lightest?

Orange Juice

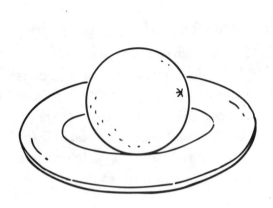

1. Put an orange on a plate.

2. Slice the orange in half.

3. Squeeze an orange half on the juicer.

4. Put ice in the glass.

5. Pour the juice over the ice.

6. Drink and enjoy!

Idea Bags for the Kitchen FE11036

Pea Bites

Ingredients:

    peas still in their pods

    water

Utensils:

    paper towels

    a plate

FYI:

The average harvest in the United States for dry peas is about 220,000 tons a year. Most peas are grown in Wisconsin and Washington. One pound of pea pods will yield about one cup of peas.

Tip:

If you are cooking peas, add salt halfway through the cooking process. This will prevent the peas from becoming tough.

Questions to ask your child while cooking:

1. Why do you think we first washed the pea pod?

2. Before you open the pod, how many peas do you think will be inside? What color will they be? Let's see!

3. How do you think the peas taste after they are cooked? What color will they be then?

4. Pretend you are a pea in a pod. What would you look like? How would you feel? How could you get out?

Cut along dashed line and glue to a brown paper lunch bag.

While preparing this recipe, your child is learning:

1. Science skills. Making predictions is a basic science skill. Your child can make predictions by guessing the number of peas in a pod before opening it, then checking the prediction and counting the peas inside. Your child will also reinforce that plants make seeds from which new plants will grow. In this case, the pea is actually the seed of the pea plant.

2. Math skills. Your child can count and compare the numbers of peas inside pods, as well as compare the peas for size. Your child can practice estimating by guessing how many peas are in a bowl, then counting the peas to check his or her estimate.

3. Language skills. Reinforce position words by having your child decide if the peas are inside or outside of the pea pod.

4. Reading skill. Read the recipe with your child. Help him or her recognize the repeated words *the pea pod*. Using picture clues, encourage your child to fill in the new beginning word of each sentence as you read the recipe a second time.

Cooking vocabulary to share with your child:

petits fours: small, fancy cakes and biscuits

poach: a method of cooking food, like an egg, by simmering the food on top of water

Idea Bags for the Kitchen

Fun activities to do with your child

1. Place all the pea pods in a bowl. Invite your child to estimate how many pods there are. Write down the number. With your child, count the pods and compare the number with his or estimate. You could repeat the activity by inviting your child to estimate the number of peas, too.

2. As you and your child open the pea pods, have your child count each pod to see if each has the same amount of peas. You might start a simple graph to record what you discover. For example, draw several columns on a sheet of paper. Label the columns 1 pea, 2 peas, 3 peas, and so on. Make a tally in the appropriate column to record the number of peas in a pod. Compare the columns to determine which amount of peas was most common.

3. Point out to your child that a pea is green. Challenge your child to recall other green vegetables, such as spinach, green beans, broccoli, lettuce, cucumbers, and asparagus. You might have your child draw these green foods. Help your child label the drawings.

4. Share with your child that a pea is actually the seed of the pea plant. To prove it, plant a raw pea in some potting soil. Make sure it gets enough water and sunlight. With your child, observe as the pea plant begins to grow.

Idea Bags for the Kitchen FE11036

Pea Bites

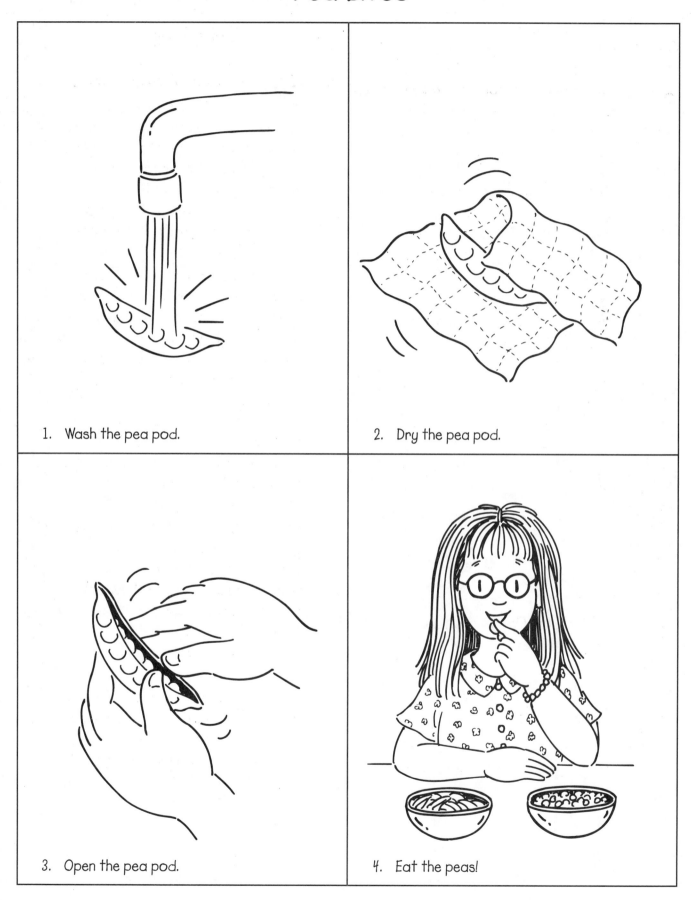

1. Wash the pea pod.

2. Dry the pea pod.

3. Open the pea pod.

4. Eat the peas!

Idea Bags for the Kitchen FE11036

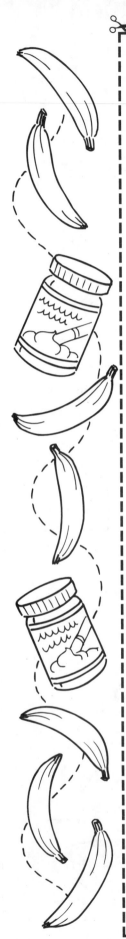
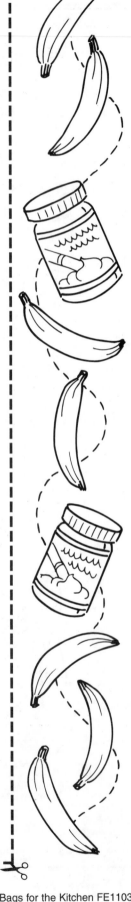

Peanut-Butter-and-Banana Shake

Ingredients:
   1/4 cup of peanut butter
   2 cups of vanilla yogurt
   1 cup of milk
   1 banana

Utensils:
   a blender
   measuring cups
   drinking cups
   a dull knife

FYI:

Bananas originated in Malaysia about 4,000 years ago. Travelers carried bananas eastward throughout the Pacific, and westward across the Indian Ocean to tropical Africa. Europeans brought the banana to the Americas.

Tip:

Put a little vegetable oil in the measuring cup before you put in the peanut butter. This will help the peanut butter slide more easily into the bowl. (You can also use nonstick spray.)

Questions to ask your child while cooking:

1. Why do you think this recipe needs milk?
2. What made the peanut butter become a liquid?
3. How is the shake different from its original ingredients?
4. What happened to the banana?
5. How many ingredients in all did we use to make this shake?

Cut along dashed line and glue to a brown paper lunch bag.

Idea Bags for the Kitchen FE11036

While preparing this recipe, your child is learning:

1. **Science skills.** As your child describes how foods taste, smell, look, and feel, your child is becoming aware of the five senses. Your child can also identify solid foods and liquid foods, comparing their different properties. (Solids have an absolute shape. Liquids change their shape according to the container they are in.)

2. **Language skills.** As your child adds each ingredient, your child will be learning new vocabulary, using describing words, and identifying sounds.

3. **Math skills.** This recipe sharpens your child's ability to measure and count, as well as to make comparisons.

4. **Reading skills.** Several recipe steps have more than one sentence. Help your child recognize where one sentence ends and another begins. This is a basic concept of print.

Cooking vocabulary to share with your child:

gastronomy: the art and science of eating

grate: to rub food on a tool that shreds, or grates, it into fine pieces.

Idea Bags for the Kitchen

Fun activities to do with your child

1. Let your child try the same recipe, substituting a different fruit for the banana. Have your child compare the shakes and comment on their similar and different flavors.

2. Encourage your child to talk about the cooking process in terms of sensory words. For example, what colors are the foods? What color is the final shake? What do the foods smell like? What does the shake smell like? How does each ingredient taste? How does the shake taste? How does each ingredient feel to the touch? How does the shake feel?

3. As you and your child watch the blender mix the ingredients, suggest that your child use a watch or clock to time how long it takes before all the ingredients are blended.

4. Line up three or four bananas. Challenge your child to arrange the bananas in order of size, from shortest to longest.

5. Visit your local library to obtain a copy of *Milk Makers* by Gail Gibbons (Aladdin Paperbacks, 1985). Read the book with your child.

Peanut-Butter-and-Banana Shake

1. Measure 1/4 cup of peanut butter. Put it in the blender.

2. Measure 2 cups of yogurt. Put it in the blender.

3. Measure 1 cup of milk. Put it in the blender.

4. Slice a banana.

5. Put the banana in the blender.

6. Put on the blender lid. Turn on the blender.

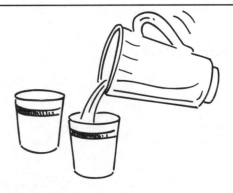

7. Pour the shake into cups.

8. Drink and enjoy!

Idea Bags for the Kitchen FE11036

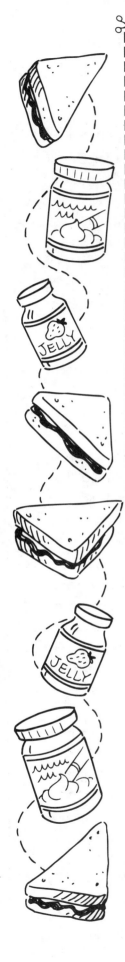
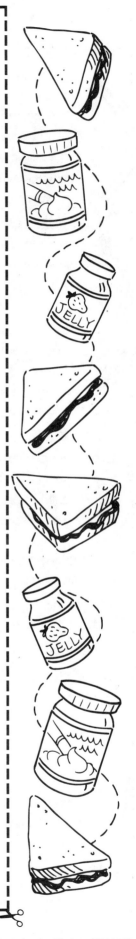

Peanut-Butter-and-Jelly Sandwich

Ingredients:
  peanut butter
  jelly
  bread

Utensils:
  a dull knife
  a plate

FYI:

Jelly is made from clear fruit juice. To make jam, however, the juice and fruit pulp are used together. You can tell the difference between jam and jelly because jam is usually more lumpy and cloudy than jelly.

Tip:

Peanut butter is easier to spread if you set the jar in a pan of hot water for a few minutes so the peanut butter softens.

Questions to ask your child while cooking:

1. What is your favorite flavor of jelly? Why?
2. How much peanut butter do you think we used in the sandwich?
3. How many layers does your sandwich have?
4. What would the sandwich look like if it were cut in two equal parts? What shapes could the parts be? (triangles or rectangles)
5. Do you think the sandwich will taste different when it is cut in half? Why or why not?
6. What other ingredient could you add to your sandwich?

Cut along dashed line and glue to a brown paper lunch bag.

While preparing this recipe, your child is learning:

1. Fine-motor skills. Spreading the peanut butter and the jelly improves your child's small-muscle skills. This is precision work for your child, and it will help when your child writes numbers and letters.

2. Writing skills. Your child will practice writing skills as he or she lists the ingredients in the peanut-butter-and-jelly sandwich.

3. Math skills. Counting and comparing skills are sharpened as your child figures out how many crackers equal the size of one slice of bread. Fractions are also used when cutting a whole sandwich in half or quarters.

4. Reading skills. Your child will start to recognize words on jam, jelly, and peanut-butter labels. Encourage your child to notice and "read" these examples of environmental print.

Cooking vocabulary to share with your child:

combine: to mix ingredients of a recipe together

confectionery: a branch of cookery where sugar is transformed into decorative sweets

Idea Bags for the Kitchen

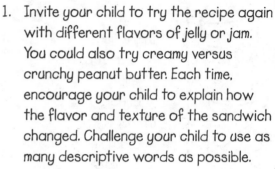

Fun activities to do with your child

1. Invite your child to try the recipe again with different flavors of jelly or jam. You could also try creamy versus crunchy peanut butter. Each time, encourage your child to explain how the flavor and texture of the sandwich changed. Challenge your child to use as many descriptive words as possible.

2. Instead of jelly, suggest that your child try honey on the sandwich. Have your child compare the flavor of the honey sandwich to a jelly sandwich. Which does your child prefer? Why?

3. On a large sheet of paper, draw a large sandwich shape. Cut it out. Help your child write the ingredients of the peanut-butter-and-jelly sandwich within the cutout. Let your child decorate the list with pictures.

4. Instead of bread, let your child make the sandwich with crackers. Have your child compare the size of the cracker sandwich to the size of the bread sandwich. Let your child place crackers on top of the bread to determine how many crackers equal one slice of bread.

5. Encourage your child to think creatively to come up with a fourth ingredient for the sandwich. Which other food could be added? Let your child try his or her suggestions. For example: raisins, banana slices, potato chips, jelly beans, different types of nuts, or chocolate chips might be added to the sandwich. Help your child add another step to the recipe to include the new ingredient.

Peanut-Butter-and-Jelly Sandwich

1. Spread peanut butter on 1 slice of bread.

2. Spread jelly on another slice of bread.

3. Put the slices of bread together.

4. Eat and enjoy!

Idea Bags for the Kitchen FE11036

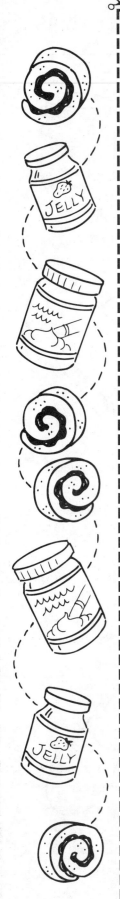
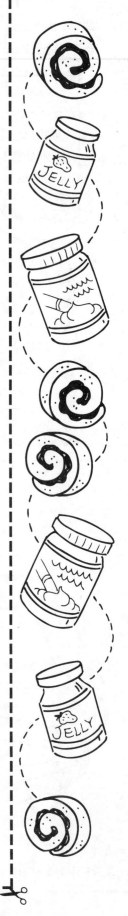

Peanut-Butter Pinwheels

Ingredients:
- peanut butter
- bread

Utensils:
- a cutting board
- a rolling pin
- a dull knife

FYI:

The peanut is an edible seed of the peanut plant. It belongs to the food family called legumes, which includes the pea and all beans. The peanut plant is unusual because the peanut pods grow underground. For this reason, peanuts are sometimes called groundnuts. Other names for peanuts include goobers, mami, archides, and pinders, although they are not commonly used.

Tip:

To help the peanut butter slide more easily off the knife, spray the knife with nonstick cooking spray.

Questions to ask your child while cooking:

1. What tools are we using as we cook?
2. How do the tools help us to do each job?
3. How many slices did you make from your pinwheel roll?
4. What do you think makes the bread larger?
5. What do you think the word *pinwheel* means?

Cut along dashed line and glue to a brown paper lunch bag.

Idea Bags for the Kitchen FE11036

While preparing this recipe, your child is learning:

1. Science skills. The rolling pin is an example of a wheel and axle, which is one of the seven simple machines. Point out to your child that using the rolling pin makes work easier, which is the purpose of all machines. Watching the peanut sprout will reinforce that the peanut is a seed.

2. Math skills. Your child practices counting skills by counting the number of pinwheel slices made from the rolled bread. Write down the number so your child can associate the print form with the amount.

3. Social skills. Because several peanut-butter pinwheels are made, your child can be encouraged to share this fun snack with friends and family.

4. Creative-thinking skills. Your child is thinking creatively when he or she sees the connection between an actual pinwheel and the peanut-butter pinwheels.

Cooking vocabulary to share with your child:

caramelize: to change sugar into a brown sweet liquid by heating

cream: to beat ingredients until they are soft and fluffy

Idea Bags for the Kitchen

Fun activities to do with your child

1. Make other pinwheels by substituting jams, jellies, cheese spreads, and sandwich meats. Let your child decide which ingredients to use. Have your child compare the taste and texture of the new pinwheels with the peanut-butter pinwheel. Ask your child which pinwheel he or she enjoys more. Why?

2. In a toaster oven or a regular oven, toast the pinwheels slightly until they are lightly brown. Again, have your child compare the taste and texture of the toasted pinwheels with the regular pinwheels. What does your child like about them? Is there anything your child doesn't like?

3. Show your child a pinwheel toy. Have your child make the connection between the pinwheel toy and the peanut-butter pinwheel. Why does your child think the recipe is called a pinwheel? How does the food look like a pinwheel? Let your child have fun with the toy pinwheel, blowing on it or letting the wind blow it to see how it moves.

4. Remind your child that a peanut is the seed of the peanut plant. To prove it, wet a paper towel and place it inside a resealable plastic baggie. Place a raw peanut, still in its shell, inside the baggie on the wet paper towel. Close the baggie. Over the next few days, invite your child to watch as the peanut seed begins to sprout. Be sure to keep the towel moist so the seed has water.

Idea Bags for the Kitchen FE11036

Peanut-Butter Pinwheels

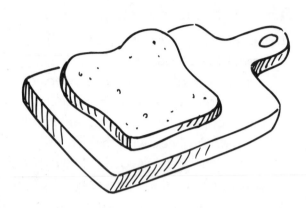

1. Place the bread on a cutting board.

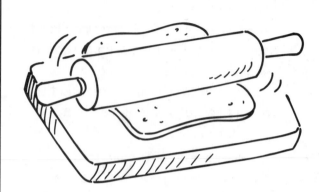

2. Roll the bread flat.

3. Spread peanut butter on the bread.

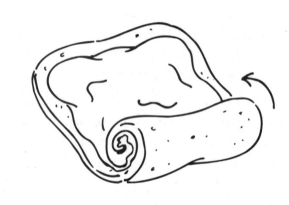

4. Roll up the bread.

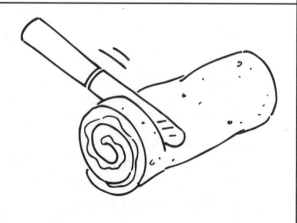

5. Slice the bread.

6. Eat and enjoy!

Idea Bags for the Kitchen FE11036

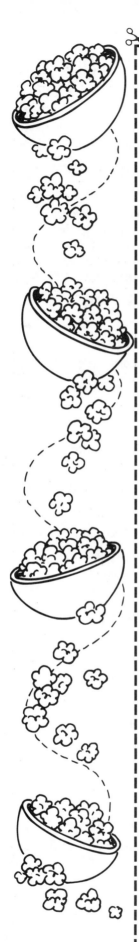

Popcorn

Ingredients:

10 tablespoons of unpopped popcorn kernels

3 tablespoons of oil

Utensils:

an electric skillet   bowl(s)

FYI:

Types of corn are classified principally on the characteristics of the corn kernels. Popcorn is one such classification. One of the oldest types of corn is flour corn. However, pod corn is probably the oldest. It is not used for food today, but mainly for scientific research.

Tip:

For fluffy popcorn, store the unpopped kernels in the freezer.

Did You Know:

People in some cultures believe that when corn kernels are popped, tiny spirits are released. In these myths, the spirits are sent to grow new food. The spirits show their gratitude by leaving behind the popped corn.

Questions to ask your child while cooking:

1. What sounds do you hear while the popcorn is popping? Let me hear you make those sounds.

2. What were the kernels like before they cooked? What are they like now? Which was smaller—the uncooked kernels or the cooked kernels?

3. Remember—corn kernels are found on a corncob. How do you think corn kernels are made into popcorn?

4. How are the unpopped popcorn kernels like the kernels of corn on an ear of corn you eat? (They are small; they have a similar rounded shape.) How are they different? (One is hard, one is soft; one is brown, one is yellow, for example.)

Cut along dashed line and glue to a brown paper lunch bag.

While preparing this recipe, your child is learning:

1. Science skills. As your child cooks the popcorn, your child will gain an understanding of cause-and-effect relationships, as well as discover how heat can change objects and substances.

2. Social studies skills. By sharing the "Did You Know" with your child, you are broadening your child's perspective and appreciation for other cultures.

3. Math skills. As your child follows this recipe, he or she will be measuring, counting, and timing. Your child can also sort different popcorns, and divide popcorn into equal quantities for sharing.

4. Oral-language skills. Your child will build oral-language skills as he or she tells the story about a popcorn spirit, as suggested in the myth from "Did You Know." By tape-recording your child's storytelling, your child can hear his or her own words played back. This activity also fosters creative-thinking skills.

Cooking vocabulary to share with your child:

napery: table linen, like a tablecloth or a napkin

overlap: to lay one piece of food partially over the other

Idea Bags for the Kitchen

Fun activities to do with your child

1. With your child, pop several bowls of popcorn. Sprinkle different toppings on the popcorn for your child to try, such as Parmesan cheese, melted butter, melted caramel. Have your child compare the flavors, then express which popcorn topping she or he prefers. Why?

2. Visit your local library to obtain a copy of the book *The Popcorn Dragon* by Jane Thayer (Morrow, Wiliam, and Co., 1991). Read it with your child.

3. Review the popcorn myth in "Did You Know." Work with your child to write an actual story based on this myth. Suggest that your child come up with a popcorn-spirit character, as well as a human or animal character that witnesses the spirit being released. Tape-record your child as she or he tells the story. Invite your child to draw pictures of the story, then share the recording and the pictures with family or friends.

4. Mix colored popcorn with natural-colored popcorn in a large bowl. Set up several smaller bowls, one for each color. Encourage your child to sort the popcorn by color, placing the same-color popcorn in the same bowl. Afterward, you might have your child count the popcorn, write the numbers, then determine which colors have more popcorn.

Popcorn

1. Pour 10 tablespoons of popcorn kernels in the skillet.

2. Add 3 tablespoons of oil to the skillet.

3. Put the lid on the skillet.

4. Turn on the heat.

5. Listen to the popcorn pop.

6. Listen for the last pop. Count to 5.

7. Pour the popcorn into a bowl.

8. Eat and enjoy!

Idea Bags for the Kitchen FE11036

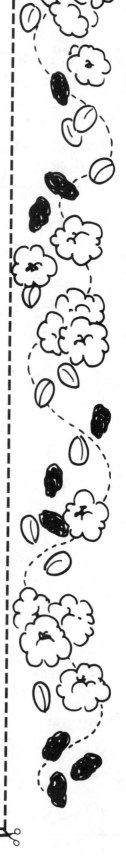

Popcorn Mix

Ingredients:

1 quart of popped popcorn
1/2 cup of unsalted peanuts
1/2 cup of raisins
2 tablespoons of peanut butter

Utensils:

measuring spoons
a measuring cup
a stove burner
a bowl
a mixing spoon

FYI:

Popcorn is a form of flint corn. It pops because the outer layer of the kernel is tough and elastic. Heat builds up inside the kernel. When the pressure from the heat finally becomes too high, the kernel pops open.

Tip:

A half cup of unpopped corn kernels makes 1 quart of popcorn.

Questions to ask your child while cooking:

1. Without looking in the pot or at the recipe, do you remember all the ingredients in our popcorn mix? Name them.

2. Why did we melt the peanut butter?

3. After cooking, how are the ingredients different? How did they change?

4. What words could you use to describe the taste and texture of the popcorn mix?

Cut along dashed line and glue to a brown paper lunch bag.

Idea Bags for the Kitchen FE11036

While preparing this recipe, your child is learning:

1. Creative-thinking skills. Your child is stretching her or his imagination when coming up with ingredients for "The Great Popcorn Mix" story. Let your child have fun and enjoy the creative experience.

2. Math skills. Your child practices estimating and counting when guessing and counting the amount of popcorn kernels in a jar. You can extend the activity to include adding and subtracting skills, too.

3. Reading skills. Your child is starting to recognize that words and pictures match. Ordered events, like those of the recipe, are easier to remember than random events. Recalling events in sequence is also part of recognizing a pattern, and learning patterns is a foundation for all learning.

4. Writing skills. Your child is practicing writing when he or she writes numbers for estimating and counting. Your child is also writing words for the "Great Popcorn Mix" story.

Cooking vocabulary to share with your child:

knead: to fold and press dough with the heel of the hand

ladle: a large, long-handled spoon used to serve liquid food, such as soup and gravy

Idea Bags for the Kitchen

Fun activities to do with your child

1. Put a handful of unpopped corn kernels in a see-through jar. Challenge your child to estimate how many kernels are in the jar. Ask your child to write down the number. Pour out the kernels, and help your child count them. You can draw a number line along a sheet of paper, then have your child place one kernel at each number on the line.

2. To extend the above activity, set up addition and subtraction problems with the kernels. For example, spread out 10 kernels. Take away two. Ask your child how many kernels remain.

3. Have your child write a story about "The Great Popcorn Mix." Ask your child to imagine a mix so big that it can feed a whole town. Would the mix be made in a cement mixer? What ingredients would it include? Ask your child to think of as many details as possible. Let your child have fun describing the preparation of the mix, and creating characters to enjoy the creation. Help your child write the words for the story, or write them yourself as your child dictates. You might tape-record your child's story so he or she can enjoy the tale again.

4. Tell your child that raisins actually begin as grapes. To prove it, set several grapes on a plate on a sunny windowsill. Check the grapes every few hours to see how they change. (Hint: To keep ants away, draw a chalk line around the plate. The ants won't cross the chalk line.)

71
reproducible

Idea Bags for the Kitchen FE11036

Popcorn Mix

1. Measure 1 quart of popped popcorn. Put it in a large bowl.

2. Measure 1/2 cup of peanuts. Put it in the bowl.

3. Measure 1/2 cup of raisins. Put it in the bowl.

4. Measure 2 tablespoons of peanut butter. Put it in a pot.

5. Melt the peanut butter on the stove.

6. Pour the melted peanut butter over the food in the bowl.

7. Mix the food in the bowl.

8. Eat and enjoy!

Idea Bags for the Kitchen FE11036

Pumpkin Pancakes

Ingredients:

4 cups of pancake mix

1 cup of canned pumpkin

1 teaspoon of cinnamon

2 eggs

honey (optional)

butter or margarine (optional)

Utensils:

measuring cups   measuring spoons

a large bowl   a large mixing spoon

a spatula   plates and forks

an electric skillet or frying pan

FYI:

Pumpkins grow on a vine that runs along the ground, and they have large, prickly leaves. The plant produces both male and female flowers. The male flower has the pollen. Bees and insects transfer the pollen to the female flower as they visit each flower, looking for food. Once pollinated, a pumpkin starts to grow inside the female flower.

Tip:

The pumpkin pancakes will dry quickly if not eaten within 15 to 30 minutes after cooking. To keep them warm, put them on a cookie sheet layered with a paper towel. Cover with a lightweight kitchen towel. Place the pancakes in an oven at 200°F. Check the pancakes frequently while in the oven.

Questions to ask your child while cooking:

1. What were the ingredients of the pumpkin pancakes?

2. What other types of pancakes have you eaten?

3. How did the pancake batter change as it cooked? Why do you think this happened?

4. Which do you like best–the pancakes with butter or the pancakes with honey?

Cut along dashed line and glue to a brown paper lunch bag.

Idea Bags for the Kitchen FE11036

While you are cooking, your child is learning:

1. Math skills. Your child will become aware of the numbers used as she or he measures quantities. Math also comes into play when your child compares and measures pumpkin sizes.

2. Science skills. As your child cooks the pumpkin pancakes, your child observes as a liquid (the batter) turns into a solid (the pancakes) through heating.

3. Social skills. Because this recipe requires a stove or skillet, your child will need to do much of the cooking with you. This will foster a sense of cooperation and working with others.

4. Language skills. As your child follows the recipe directions, she or he will be performing various tasks, such as mixing, adding, pouring, and flipping. Your child will become familiar with these terms, building language skills.

Cooking vocabulary to share with your child:

pare or peel: to remove the outer skin of a food

pinch: a very small amount of an ingredient that can be held between the thumb and index finger

Idea Bags for the Kitchen

Fun activities to do with your child

1. Line up several pumpkins of different sizes on a table or counter in any order. Challenge your child to arrange the pumpkins by size, from smallest to largest.

2. Help your child measure the circumference of each pumpkin. With your child, wrap some string around the pumpkin's middle. Cut the string to show the proper width. Repeat the procedure with several other pumpkins of various sizes. Then have your child compare the string lengths. Help your child conclude that the longer strings represent the bigger pumpkins. Have your child measure the strings with a ruler or tape measure and write down the numbers.

3. Visit your local library to obtain a copy of *The Vanishing Pumpkin* by Tony Johnston (Putnam Publishing, 1996). Read it with your child.

4. Make a pumpkin book with your child. Cut out a pumpkin shape from orange paper to serve as the cover. Cut out several sheets of white paper, the same size and shape as the cover, to be the book pages. Encourage your child to draw pictures of the pumpkins at your home, along with any pumpkin carvings you might have done.

Pumpkin Pancakes

1. Mix 4 cups of pancake mix and 1 teaspoon of cinnamon in a bowl.

2. Add 2 eggs.

3. Add 1 cup of pumpkin.

4. Stir well.

5. Pour small circles of batter into the skillet.

6. Wait for bubbles to form on the pancakes.

7. Flip the pancakes. Cook the other side.

8. Add butter or honey. Eat and enjoy!

Idea Bags for the Kitchen FE11036

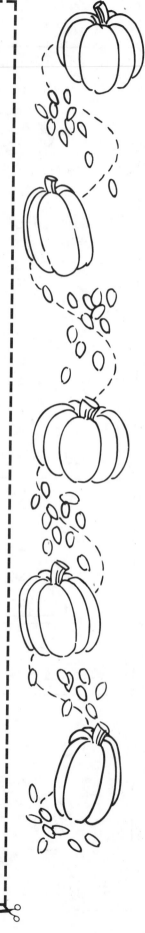

Pumpkin Seeds

Ingredients:
    pumpkins
    1 cup of pumpkin seeds
    1 tablespoon of vegetable oil
    salt

Utensils:
    an oven
    a measuring spoon
    a measuring cup
    a cookie sheet

FYI:

Pumpkins grow from seeds found inside the pumpkin. The seeds are planted in groups called hills. The well-known orange pumpkin is not harvested until the skin is tough—about 120 days after planting. Pumpkins must be picked before the first frost.

Tip:

Wash the seeds carefully and put them on a piece of wax paper to dry. Blot them occasionally with a paper towel. The seeds will cook better if they dry overnight.

Questions to ask your child while cooking:

1. What do you think will happen when the pumpkin seeds are baked in the oven?

2. Where could we find information about pumpkins and pumpkin seeds?

3. How many seeds do you think are inside a pumpkin? How could you find out?

4. Why do we cook the pumpkin seeds in oil? What does the oil do?

5. Why do we sprinkle the pumpkin seeds with salt? What does the salt do?

Cut along dashed line and glue to a brown paper lunch bag.

Idea Bags for the Kitchen FE11036

While preparing this recipe, your child is learning:

1. Math skills. This recipe encourages your child to practice measuring quantities and to recognize the time span of 10 minutes. The additional activities encourage your child to practice adding, subtracting, and comparing.

2. Reading skills. As your child follows the recipe on the page, he or she is becoming aware that words have meaning. Point out to your child that the words give information about the pictures.

3. Social skills. The abundance of baked pumpkins seeds will encourage your child to share the snack with others.

4. Science skills. As your child removes seeds from the pumpkin, your child will recall that seeds of a plant are found inside the fruit of the plant. Planting the seeds will reinforce the life cycle of a plant.

Cooking vocabulary to share with your child:

mince: to cut a food into very small pieces

moisten: to add a liquid, usually water, to a food

Idea Bags for the Kitchen

Fun activities to do with your child

1. If you obtained your pumpkin seeds from pumpkins, invite your child to paint faces on the pumpkins. With close supervision, your child may be able to carve a jack o' lantern.

2. Invite your child to count the pumpkin seeds on the cookie sheet. Write down the number. Then ask your child to group the seeds into equal piles (for example, piles with 4 seeds each; piles with 10 seeds each). Talk with your child about the number of piles made with each grouping. For additional math activities, make up story problems with your child as you share the seeds. For example, "I am eating 3 of your seeds. How many seeds do you have left?"

3. Visit your local library to obtain a copy of *Our Pumpkin* by Renee Keeler (Creative Teaching Press, 1996). Read it with your child.

4. Sprout a pumpkin plant with some of the uncooked seeds. Leave the seeds on a sunny windowsill to dry for two days. Place a wet sponge in a shallow bowl. Set the seeds on the sponge. Keep the sponge wet, and invite your child to watch as the seeds sprout.

Idea Bags for the Kitchen FE11036

Pumpkin Seeds

1. Put 1 cup of pumpkin seeds in a bowl.

2. Mix in 1 tablespoon of oil.

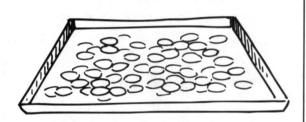

3. Spread the seeds on a cookie sheet.

4. Set a timer for 10 minutes. Bake the seeds at 375°F.

5. Sprinkle the seeds with salt.

6. Eat and enjoy!

Idea Bags for the Kitchen FE11036

Pumpkin Shake

Ingredients:
- 5 scoops of ice cream
- 5 tablespoons of pumpkin fruit
- 2-1/2 cups of milk
- a dash of cinnamon

Utensils:
- an ice-cream scooper
- measuring cups
- measuring spoons
- a blender
- glasses
- straws

FYI:

Jacob Fussel established the first ice-cream factory in 1851 in Baltimore, Maryland. His success led to the development of ice-cream producers throughout the United States. The ice-cream soda was introduced in 1879. The ice-cream cone appeared in 1904 at the World's Fair in St. Louis, Missouri.

Tip:

To get the pumpkin to slide out of the measuring cup, first spray the cup lightly with nonstick cooking spray.

Questions to ask your child while cooking:

1. What ingredients went into the shake?
2. Which ingredient made the shake cold?
3. What color did the shake become? Why?
4. How are ice cream and milk alike? (They are both dairy products, for example.) How are they different?
5. What tools did we use to make the shake?
6. How did the tools help us?

Cut along dashed line and glue to a brown paper lunch bag.

Idea Bags for the Kitchen FE11036

While preparing this recipe, your child is learning:

1. Math skills. While making the pumpkin shake, your child is encouraged to recognize color; to measure quantities, and to divide the shake into equal amounts.

2. Reading skills. Part of reading comprehension is recalling sequence, or the order in which events happen. Your child can practice sequencing by recalling the steps of the recipe in order.

3. Creative-thinking skills. Creativity will be strengthened when your child is asked to tell a story about a pumpkin waiting to be picked in a pumpkin patch.

4. Science skills. Your child is experiencing cause-and-effect relationships. For example, when pumpkin is added to the ice-cream mixture, it changes color. Your child also observes how objects can change shape.

Cooking vocabulary to share with your child:

fry: to cook a food in hot oil

garnish: to add trimmings to a food for taste and visual appeal

Idea Bags for the Kitchen

Fun activities to do with your child

1. With your child, visit a local library. Help your child locate and check out the book *Pumpkin, Pumpkin* by Jean Titherighton (Morrow, William, and Co., 1990). Read the book with your child.

2. Invite your child to consider what it might be like to be a pumpkin sitting in a pumpkin patch, waiting to be picked. How might the pumpkin feel when it is brought home? How might the pumpkin feel when it is decorated for the holidays? Encourage your child to think creatively and to tell a story about the pumpkin. As your child speaks, write down her or his ideas. This will also reinforce the connection between the written and the spoken word. Read back your child's story aloud. Then invite your child to draw pictures to go with it.

3. Let your child draw faces on a pumpkin. You may do so with markers or paints. You might use the pumpkin to inspire your child's storytelling for the above activity.

4. With your child, make a pumpkin rubbing. Cover one side of a pumpkin with orange paint. Press a piece of paper over the paint and rub gently. The textured pumpkin surface will appear on the paper.

Idea Bags for the Kitchen FE11036

Pumpkin Shake

1. Gather the ingredients and cooking tools.

2. Put 5 scoops of ice cream in the blender.

3. Put 5 tablespoons of pumpkin fruit in the blender.

4. Put 2-1/2 cups of milk in the blender.

5. Put a dash of cinnamon in the blender.

6. Put on the blender lid. Blend.

7. Pour the pumpkin shake into cups.

8. Drink and enjoy!

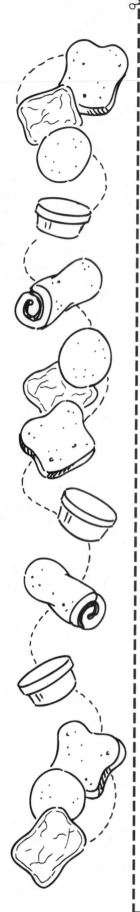

Sandwich Roll

Ingredients:
- cream cheese
- turkey slices
- ham slices
- bread

Utensils:
- a plate
- a dull knife

FYI:

The sandwich was named after John Montagu, the Earl of Sandwich. Montagu was a gambler. In order to continue gambling without stopping to cut and eat his food, he requested a single dish in which the meat and bread could be eaten quickly together.

Tip:

To spread the cream cheese, try using a jumbo craft stick instead of a knife. This is especially helpful if several children are cooking. Since children often like to lick the spreader, using a disposable spreader means each child can have his or her own.

Did Your Know:

The sandwich is one of the most popular foods eaten in the United States, especially with children ages 2 to 10.

Questions to ask your child while cooking:

1. How is the sandwich roll like a regular sandwich? How is it different?
2. How many foods did you put on your sandwich?
3. How else could you make this sandwich?
4. Which do you like best—turkey or ham?

Cut along dashed line and glue to a brown paper lunch bag.

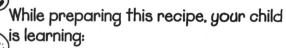

While preparing this recipe, your child is learning:

1. Math skills. Your child is identifying shapes, such as bread and meat slices, and the cylindrical shape of the sandwich roll.

2. Fine-motor skills. The rolling motion used to form the sandwich roll requires your child to utilize the small muscles of the hands, which will improve dexterity for writing.

3. Science skills. Understanding food and nutrition is a science topic. Reviewing the levels of the food pyramid and the suggested quantities of each food strengthens your child's understanding of food groups.

4. Writing skills. By copying the recipe and inserting new ingredients, your child is practicing forming letters and writing sentences.

Cooking vocabulary to share with your child:

cube: to cut food into six-sided, cube-shaped pieces

culinary: the art and practice of preparing and cooking

Idea Bags for the Kitchen

Fun activities to do with your child

1. Talk with your child about why the ingredients for the sandwich roll are able to be rolled up. Invite your child on a scavenger hunt around your home for objects than can be rolled up. Some ideas to explore include maps, rugs, blankets, posters, and so on. If possible, let your child have fun rolling up each object. Compare how the shape and size of the objects changed when rolled.

2. Let your child substitute other meats or spreads in the sandwich-roll recipe. Help your child rewrite the recipe to reflect the new ingredients. Have your child copy the words from the recipe sheet onto writing paper. When you come to the words *ham, turkey,* and *cream cheese,* tell your child how to spell the new ingredients to write in their place. Read the recipe back with your child.

3. Share with your child that the foods in the sandwich roll represent three of the six food groups. Bread is part of the grain group. Cream cheese is part of the dairy group. Ham and turkey are part of the meat group. The remaining groups are fruits, vegetables, and sugars. Let your child have fun adding three more foods to include all the food groups.

4. Some food packages have an illustrated food pyramid near the ingredients or nutrition listings. Find a food pyramid on a food package and read it with your child. Talk about the foods and food quantities that make up a healthy diet.

Sandwich Roll

1. Put a slice of bread on a plate.

2. Spread some cream cheese on the bread.

3. Put a slice of ham on the bread.

4. Put a slice of turkey on the ham.

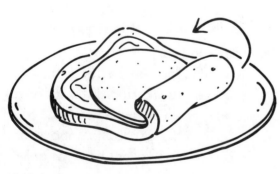

5. Roll it up.

6. Eat and enjoy!

Idea Bags for the Kitchen FE11036

Snow Cone

Ingredients:
ice cubes
water
several flavors of fruit-juice frozen concentrate
(orange, grape, lemonade, for example)

Utensils:
a blender
a measuring cup
a plastic or paper drinking cup

FYI:

Snow cones were originally called "water ices" or sherbets. They were eaten between courses of a meal to clear the eater's palate. The ices were often served in special decorative glasses. In France, they are called sorbets.

Tip:

Before beginning this recipe, defrost the fruit-juice concentrate. Prepare the fruit juice, using only half the water directed. This will make the juice thicker and more enjoyable as a snow-cone treat.

Questions to ask your child while cooking:

1. What shape is the ice before it goes into the blender?
2. How many ice cubes did we use?
3. How does the ice change in the blender?
4. How is the snow cone like a Popsicle? How is it like ice cream?
5. What juice did we use?
6. How did the juice change the ice?

Cut along dashed line and glue to a brown paper lunch bag.

Idea Bags for the Kitchen FE11036

When preparing this recipe, your child is learning:

1. Math skills. This recipe encourages your child to count ice cubes and consider quantities in reference to more than or less than.

2. Science skills. Help your child realize that frozen ice cubes are an example of the solid form that matter can take. As the ice melts, point out that the water left behind is the liquid form of matter.

3. Language skills. When saying the words *snow cone*, your child hears the long-o sound. Your child will have fun playing with language as she or he comes up with tongue twisters with other words that have the long-o sound. Reciting the tongue twisters to others also sharpens oral-language skills.

4. Creative-thinking skills. By brainstorming fun names for the snow-cone creations, your child practices creative thinking.

Cooking vocabulary to share with your child:

drain: to pour off liquid, drop by drop; or to let a liquid drain in a sieve or colander

entrée: the main course of a meal

Idea Bags for the Kitchen

Fun activities to do with your child

1. Speculate with your child other methods for crushing the ice. Let your child try those that he or she suggests. Other ways could include crushing the ice with a hammer, shredding it with a large cheese grater, or using an ice crusher. (If using a hammer, wrap the ice in a towel before striking.) Have your child compare the ice chips created by the different methods.

2. While making the snow cone, have your child repeat the words *snow cone*. Point out that the words have the same vowel sound—long o. Help your child create silly tongue twisters with other words that have the long-o sound. For example: The toad stole the rosy snow cone. The old goat gloated as he rowed his boat across the moat. Write down the tongue twisters, and challenge your child to circle all the o's.

3. As your child eats the snow cone, brainstorm fun names for it. Suggest that the name includes the flavor of the snow cone. Your child could also include his or her own name. For example: the treat might be called Maria's Strawberry Ice Delight or Benny's Best Orange Freezy.

4. Dump a freezer tray full of ice cubes into a bowl. Ask your child to estimate how many cups of water the ice cubes will make when melted. Write down the number. When the ice has melted, have your child pour the water into measuring cups to check his or her estimates.

Snow Cones

1. Put the ice cubes in the blender.

2. Pour 1/4 cup of water into the blender.

3. Put the lid on the blender.

4. Turn on the blender to crush the ice.

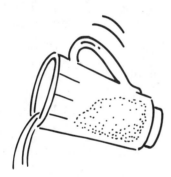

5. Drain off any extra water.

6. Pour the ice into a cup.

7. Pour the fruit juice over the ice.

8. Eat and enjoy!

Idea Bags for the Kitchen FE11036

Strawberry Yogurt

Ingredients:

about 5 strawberries

a small carton of plain yogurt

Utensils:

a cutting board   a dull knife   a spoon

FYI:

Unlike most berries, strawberries carry their seeds on the outside of their skin. These are the small dots that give the strawberry its bumpy exterior. For this reason, scientists don't classify strawberries as true berries. True berries, like blueberries and cranberries, carry their seeds on the inside.

Tip:

Refrigerate ripe strawberries immediately after purchase. To keep them fresh as long as possible, store them in a large bowl to provide lots of space between the berries. Do not wash the strawberries or remove the leafy stems until you are ready to eat them.

Questions to ask your child while cooking:

1. What is the main color of the strawberry? What other colors do you see?

2. What do you think the tiny bumps are on the strawberry skin?

3. What words could describe the flavor of a strawberry?

4. Do all the strawberries look alike? What do they have in common? How are they different?

5. How many strawberries do you think are in the basket? How can we find out?

6. How would you describe the flavor of the strawberries and yogurt mixed together? Do you like it? Why or why not?

Cut along dashed line and glue to a brown paper lunch bag.

Idea Bags for the Kitchen FE11036

While preparing this recipe, your child is learning:

1. Math skills. Identifying colors and shapes is an early math skill. Your child will also practice counting and comparing.

2. Emotional development. Your child will not always like everything she or he eats. As your child recognizes food preferences, he or she is learning self expression and building a sense of self.

3. Science skills. This recipe encourages your child to recall to which food groups strawberries and yogurt belong. Doing this promotes categorizing skills.

4. Writing skills. By copying the recipe with a new fruit, your child is practicing the mechanics of writing. This activity is a good opportunity to point out to your child that a sentence begins with a capital letter and ends with a punctuation mark.

Cooking vocabulary to share with your child:

coat: to cover a food with another food completely, usually with flour

scallop: to bake in a sauce covered in bread or cracker crumbs or to cut in the shape of a seashell

Idea Bags for the Kitchen

Fun activities to do with your child

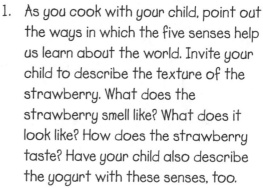

1. As you cook with your child, point out the ways in which the five senses help us learn about the world. Invite your child to describe the texture of the strawberry. What does the strawberry smell like? What does it look like? How does the strawberry taste? Have your child also describe the yogurt with these senses, too.

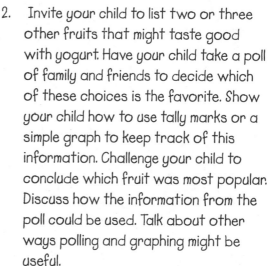

2. Invite your child to list two or three other fruits that might taste good with yogurt. Have your child take a poll of family and friends to decide which of these choices is the favorite. Show your child how to use tally marks or a simple graph to keep track of this information. Challenge your child to conclude which fruit was most popular. Discuss how the information from the poll could be used. Talk about other ways polling and graphing might be useful.

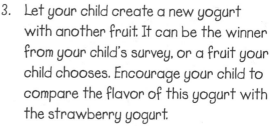

3. Let your child create a new yogurt with another fruit. It can be the winner from your child's survey, or a fruit your child chooses. Encourage your child to compare the flavor of this yogurt with the strawberry yogurt.

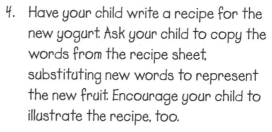

4. Have your child write a recipe for the new yogurt. Ask your child to copy the words from the recipe sheet, substituting new words to represent the new fruit. Encourage your child to illustrate the recipe, too.

Strawberry Yogurt

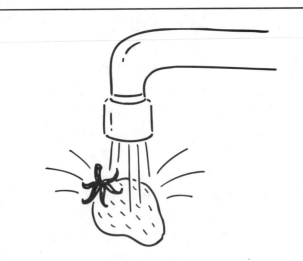

1. Wash the strawberries.

2. Pull off the leafy tops.

3. Slice the strawberries.

4. Put the strawberries in the yogurt.

5. Mix the strawberries and yogurt.

6. Eat and enjoy!

Idea Bags for the Kitchen FE11036